THE SSAC
ADVANCED DIVE TRAINING MANUAL

THE SSAC ADVANCED DIVE TRAINING MANUAL

1st Edition

1990

THE SCOTTISH SUB-AQUA CLUB

GLASGOW

Published by the Scottish Sub-Aqua Club,
40 Bogmoor Place, Glasgow

Copyright © SSAC 1990

ISBN 0 904419 03 7

Printed in Scotland by W. M. Bett Ltd., Tillicoultry

Foreword

The Scottish Sub-Aqua Club has decided to reissue its Dive Training Manual in two parts, to be known as The SSAC Introductory Dive Training Manual : elements and the SSAC Advanced Dive Training Manual. Material taking you as far as the 2nd Class Diver level is to be found in the first of these volumes.

The opportunity has been taken to modernise the content and appearance of both parts. The pagination has been changed and the index at the end of this volume refers to both parts of the Manual. Figure numbering is in sequence with the first half of the Manual. Details of the Branch Instructor Qualification are included as Chapter 9.

I am grateful to all those members who have made suggestions for the text of this publication, in particular to Peter Armstrong, NDO in 1990.

ADAM CURTIS
Editor

Contents

Chapter 1

The First Class Diver

The SSAC, like many other clubs, has found it quite easy to lay down a precise training and testing schedule for its more junior awards (3rd and 2nd Class Diver) but has never prescribed an exact schedule for its top diving award, the 1st Class certificate. Some people have found this lack of a schedule surprising and worrying but if you consider the definition of a 1st Class diver it is clear why this has been done.

The 1st Class diver is expected to know all that there is to know about the theory and practice of the type of diving undertaken by amateurs and a great deal about matters ancillary to this. These ancillary matters cover a wide range of subjects such as The History of Diving, Theory of Mixed Gas Breathing Equipment, Simple Navigation etc. Thus in a sense the basic requirement for the 1st Class award is simply a vast practical, theoretical and applied knowledge of amateur diving and as much knowledge as can be amasssed about ancillary subjects. Detailing all the knowledge as a series of tests would be exceedingly laborious and even if we were able to remember everything that would be appropriate at this moment, changes in amateur practice might render our tests out of date very rapidly. An even more important objection to defining the 1st Class award as a series of tests, whose nature is known to the diver beforehand, is that in real diving life all the unpleasant situations develop with little or no warning. Thus at some point in your diving training tests must be introduced which are not precisely specified and known to you beforehand and which require that you work out from your knowledge what is best to do.

The really good diver is characterised amongst other things by his or her ability to solve the problems in new situations which he or she may never have met before. Obviously a considerable experience of diving in a wide variety of situations with varying equipment is good training as you will have met some wide range of situations. Similarly it will be worthwhile your analysing each dive, considering whether it might not have been better or more safely carried out. Again you will find it worthwhile to analyse, discreetly perhaps, other people's dives to see how well carried out they were. All this should help to develop an ability to solve new problems easily.

Thus part of the 1st Class practical test involves the candidate in solving a series of problems about a dive. Just giving some bare hints, they might involve the best deployment of personnel, decompression situations, problems with determining slack water etc. Throughout the practical tests the candidate will be faced to a greater or lesser extent with the necessity of knowing just what is going on and how to cope with all possible developments.

Rescue situations will usually form part of the practical examination because the effective organisation of a good rescue under difficult situations is another hallmark of the wholly competent diver. Somewhat similarly the practical examination usually will contain some measure of underwater work because the 1st Class diver ought to be able to do something useful underwater, you will note that we do not ask for this in lower awards. The work will not be particularly difficult but will require some ability at construction, flotation in a controlled manner or measurement. Again the top-grade diver should be able to work in all conditions that are reasonable for amateur divers so that deep water work, low visibility work and rough water may all be conditions for the examination. Similarly he should have a wide experience of equipment such as surface demand, dry suits, full-face masks etc. and a reasonable ability at handling small hard boats and inflatables.

A 1st Class diver must also be able to supervise, control and plan for other divers in an expedition. Good divers are not loners, and very good divers are simply very good at running dives for other people.

Simple navigation comes into both the practical and theoretical examinations because a very good diver must know:

(i)   How to read charts, to judge depth, currents, and types of bottom, as well as any course laying or position finding that may be necessary;

(ii) How to read tide tables, current charts, almanacs and pilot books to calculate times of high and low water, times, strengths and directions of currents, presence of hazards;

(iii) Simple weather forecasting and judging effect of sea on small boats and divers;

(iv) Simple chartwork on courses so that you can work out either what course has been made or what course to make. Bearings and their measurement;

(v)   Meaning of flag, sound and other signals that may be relevant to diving or to work of other boats near divers. Meaning of various types of buoy.

The theoretical examinations may cover any of the points described under the practical examination but basically it tests your knowledge of the equipment, physics, physiology, good diving practice, compressor operation, and simple seamanship used in the normal conduct of SSAC club diving. To this must be added some knowledge of ancillary subjects.

A full list of ancillary subjects would include: Physics of deep diving. Advanced physiology, including such topics as decompression on gas mixtures other than air, HPNS, effects of type of diluant gas on inert gas narcosis. Other types of breathing equipment, e.g. mixed gas equipment. Testing and training divers both in SSAC and at more advanced levels. Legal aspects of diving. Gas and equipment testing. Underwater work including salvage. Advanced navigation. Elementary marine biology and marine conservation. Underwater geology and archaeology. Recording methods including photography etc.

In summary

The potential 1st Class diver should be a 2nd Class diver who:

1. Has had a considerable number (over 100) of dives under extremes of sea conditions, varying depths and weather conditions.

2. Has organised all types of diving expeditions, i.e. shore dives, boat dives, night dives, deep dives, wreck dives, mainly in the sea with varying weather and water conditions.

3. Has a thorough knowledge of the equipment he or she uses.

4. Has knowledge of all the types of equipment available to the amateur compressed air diver.

5. Has a thorough working knowledge of the physical and physiological laws of diving.

6. Is able to react quickly and efficiently to any diving situation, particularly emergency situations, making correct, sound decisions.

7. Is able to delegate responsibility in all types of situations.

8. Is fully conversant with deep dive decompression requirements, problems and back-up procedures.

9. Is able to handle a diveboat, e.g. inflatable, and is aware of the dangers of these boats with divers in and under them.

10. Is aware of the limitations of a diveboat, i.e. inflatable or hard boat.

11. Has theoretical and practical ability in handling a diveboat and a knowledge of engine problems and remedies.

12. Has a good knowledge of basic seamanship, i.e. types of boat suitable for diving, stability of boats, safety facilities on board a boat and boat accessories, launch and recovery of boats, anchoring and weighing anchor, coming alongside, departing from alongside, diver pick-up from water, rules of the road at sea, courtesy at sea, buoyage systems, chart reading and interpretation, giving aid to distressed vessels, interpretation of weather conditions, knowledge of where to seek advice regarding conditions at sea, basic knots.

13. Uses his common sense based on all of the foregoing.

The training for this qualification is arrived at by doing most, if not all, of the following:

1. Carrying out frequent dives under a wide variety of conditions.

2. Attending Advanced Diver courses.

3. Organising branch and club dives (particularly paying attention to use of charts, tide tables etc.).

4. Practising 2nd Class tests and rescues etc. from more difficult situations.

5. Thinking about how features of specific dives could have been better handled.

6. Reading diving magazines.

7. Reading widely, see Appendix on Diving Books.

Chapter 2

Training Games

Training can be fun! Although you will be required to demonstrate that you can perform specific exercises in a formal manner to your BTP, the following activities will give you the opportunity of comparing your new ability with that of trained divers. When you pass a test it is not a pinnacle of success but a plateau of achievement. It is another stage to be incorporated in the overall pattern of skills associated with diving. These skills are 'functional' and when acquired should be used in a variety of situations so that they become 'adaptive'. They should not be performed in isolation or as a programmed repertoire but as a variable sequence which can be altered to match the needs of recurring change. Individual divers have an efficiency threshold encountered under stress and these activities are designed to increase tolerance and extend the period before the onset of threshold degeneration. In other words, by doing them you become a better diver!

Remember at all times that it is dangerous to hyperventilate. It is a hazard even to think that hyperventilation should be used to enhance your performance of these exercises. Training personnel in charge of sessions during which these exercises are tried must ensure that no one hyperventilates. For those who are unaware of the meaning of the term, the definition of 'hyperventilation' is *the deliberate use of over-deep and over-rapid breathing before holding your breath.* One or two deep breaths may be permissible, more than this is hazardous because you may faint underwater if you hyperventilate.

LONG SNORKEL

A descriptive title. 1.5 metres of PVC piping, the type now normally used in the building industry, can be fitted over a snorkel and a watertight joint can be obtained by using tape at the top of the snorkel for a good fit. Two points to note: (1) you cannot clear the water from a snorkel of this length in the usual way and it has to be lifted clear and tipped out; (2) it must only be used for a couple of breaths at any one time as the air from your lungs will not receive sufficient change to avoid a CO_2 build-up – in any case you would be lucky to get even one!

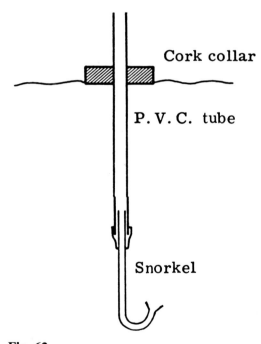

Fig. 62

This task illustrates the tremendous pressure a diver has on him even in relatively shallow water. It might be described as the reverse of conditions which could lead to lung rupture and should give the subject a far greater understanding of the lecture on the effects of pressure. It also illustrates why a 'Hookah system' must have a correctly directed non-return valve at **both** ends of the hose in case there is a loss of air supply.

If the PVC tubing is marked off in 10 cm, it makes it more interesting for the subject and a piece of cork or similar material which can slide up and down the tube acts as a stabilising float and can be used to control and record the working depth very accurately.

Never use it on your own!

SPIRO

The task is based on a scientific instrument known as a spirometer, see Fig. 63, which is used to measure the volume of air in the lungs. A four gallon plastic container with a tap at the top has its bottom cut out and spreaders fitted. The spreaders stop the sides from collapsing. The tap acts as an air vent and a weight hung from the spreaders ensures the container will float upright. The weight can be altered but 10 kg is usually found to be sufficient. The container floats in the pool as in the diagram and the subject opens the tap/vent allowing *all* the air to escape during which time the container and weight will slowly sink to the bottom. The subject holds his snorkel in his hand and dives to the container closing the vent.

The snorkel is placed against the mouth in the reverse position with the mouthpiece under the open bottom of the container. The subject blows all the air from his lungs into the container and returns to the surface repeating the process until the container and weight float once again.

When the trainee performs this task he is learning to create and cope with negative buoyancy. He is also activating and witnessing the laws of physics. If the container is marked accurately down the side and the amount of air or water level can be seen, the trainee can be asked to determine the relationship between the weight, volume of air (initial, increase and subsequent), flotation, upthrust and depth. This could follow on from his 3rd Class lectures. If the task is performed accurately on the surface in one breath, it is possible to calculate the volume of expired air and the amount of buoyancy control a subject would have and the consumption of air/cylinder contents for any given depth.

LIMBO

The activity is derived from the West Indian version and could be regarded as a high jump in reverse. A wood bar 2.5 cm × 2.5 cm × 150 cm painted black and white in alternate 10 cm sections is held by its own buoyancy against pegs in uprights at either end, see Fig.

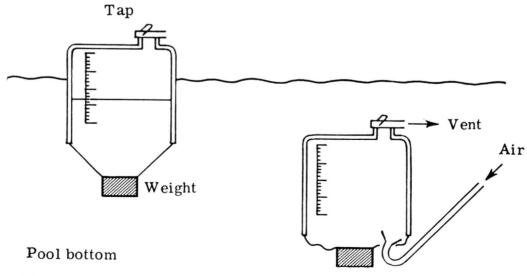

Tap

Weight

Pool bottom

Vent

Air

Fig. 63

64. The distance between the bar and pool bottom can be varied by changing the pegs in holes in the uprights. The pegs can have a cam shape as illustrated and should protrude 2.5 cm when in place. Holes 1 cm in diameter are drilled at intervals of 2 cm in the uprights which are also made of wood and held in place by weights at the base. The height of the bar can, therefore, be adjusted by 1 cm and should range from 20 cm to at least 70 cm. Round off the top of the uprights or protect them in some way to avoid any chance of injury. Make sure the subject swims under in the correct direction so that if the bar is touched it will move out from under the pegs and float to the surface. The activity can be run as a game, losing points if you dislodge the bar, either individually in a circuit or as a group activity and the manner in which it is performed can have an increasing degree of difficulty. (1) Depth of water; (2) Equipment worn: (*a*) none, (*b*) basic, (*c*) SCUBA, (*d*) full gear as in test F. It can cater for the novice or the experienced diver and it is quite easy to think up a variety of tasks with the equipment available. You are permitted to remove any gear to get under the bar but it must be replaced before surfacing. Try taking a size 5 plastic 'Frido' soccer ball under the bar at 50 cm in 2m of water with and without a weight belt!

The two main aspects in which the subject is acquiring skill in the numerous ways he performs his feats are:

1. Buoyancy control: obtaining, experiencing and controlling negative and neutral buoyancy at different depths.

2. Body awareness: control of movement and body position underwater and an awareness of the position of any equipment worn in relation to the bar and pool bottom. He will also learn to manipulate this gear to the best advantage in each situation.

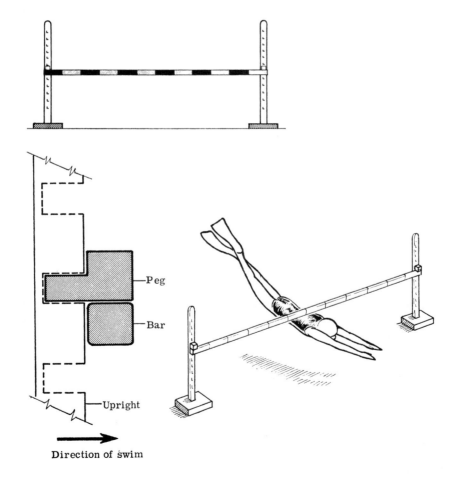

Direction of swim

Fig. 64

If the equipment for limbo is constructed accurately you can tackle pool, Branch and even Club records at your own training session.

PEGS

Properly known as 'tent pegging' the sport comes from the days of the British cavalry in India when they demonstrated their skill with the lance on horseback by spearing tent pegs at full gallop. In this case the swimmer wears basic kit and has a garden cane, old golf club shaft or GRP aerial etc. as a lance, see Fig. 65. The pegs are weighted pieces of plastic which stand upright from the bottom of the pool and have a 5 cm hole in them for spearing. They are usually set out in a straight line at intervals of 2m. The game is not meant to doom even more fish to impalement but to improve underwater vision and distance judgement. If

turning and have the number hung between these lines. There should be at least four hoops in a course and scoring is given as the total time plus penalties in seconds, see Fig. 66a.

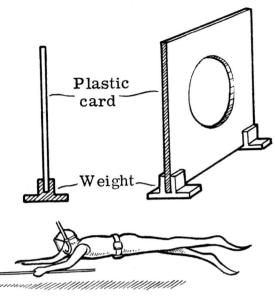

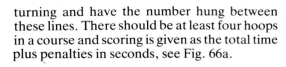

Fig. 65

the pegs have sufficient weight and the lance shaft is smooth then the subject has to swim fairly fast to hold the pegs already speared on the shaft when he lowers the end for the next one. It should help to improve finning technique and control of objects underwater. The difficulty can be varied by changing the length of the shaft between the tip and handgrip. The subject may fin in only one direction for the safety of other pool users!

SLALOM

Several numbered hoops of different diameters are held at various depths and angles in the pool. The subject swims through each hoop in a predetermined course trying not to touch any of them. In effect he is presented with a two dimensional slalom which has to be negotiated at speed requiring buoyancy control, body control, agility and breath holding. There is a time penalty of 5 seconds for every hoop touched.

The hoops are made from hose pipe filled with poly-foam or air and vary in diameter from a minimum of 50 cm to a maximum of 80 cm. They are held by two lines to prevent them

Fig. 66a

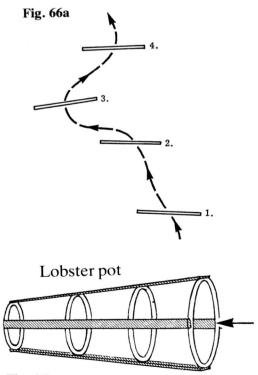

Lobster pot

Fig. 66b

LOBSTER POT

This is a particular obstacle formed by the hoops set in a straight line and linked by wood bars in descending order of diameter which gradually constricts the swimmer who must use his speed and glide action to get through. If he doesn't manage it he becomes the lobster in the pot and must back out, see Fig. 66b.

STEPPING STONES

It is not as simple as the name implies and is probably the most significant of all the activities in regard to training. Although the equipment is quite simple it can cater for all levels of ability and if properly used can form a vehicle for research purposes.

The stones are merely 5 kg weights – clean beach pebbles in a canvas bag. The bags are placed on the bottom of the pool and determine the route the subject will follow. If the bags are shaped (elongated) they can be used to provide further information about direction. The task is normally carried out with a blacked-out mask and basic kit or using SCUBA. Initially the bags are placed at double arms length apart so that the subject can feel for the next bag before relinquishing the first one. The distance between the bags can then be increased so that the subject has to 'free swim' in the correct direction for the next one. One of the bags can become an 'air station' with an aqualung placed beside it. Obstacles and 'dead ends' can be included in the courses and the amount of information available to the subject can be controlled:

1. He can see the whole route from the surface before starting.

2. He can be told the start and finish points only.

3. He can be told the start, finish and distance between.

4. He can be told the number of bags and distance between.

5. Direction can be indicated by the line of bags etc.

The task encourages the ability to think without seeing while underwater – to dive by touch, visual imagery and sense of direction. It produces problem-solving immediacy where alternatives can be offered and decisions made on a controlled information feed to the subject. In other words the subject becomes very akin to the proverbial guinea pig running a maze.

Try it using wet suit, mitts and hood!

Suitable plans are illustrated in Fig. 67.

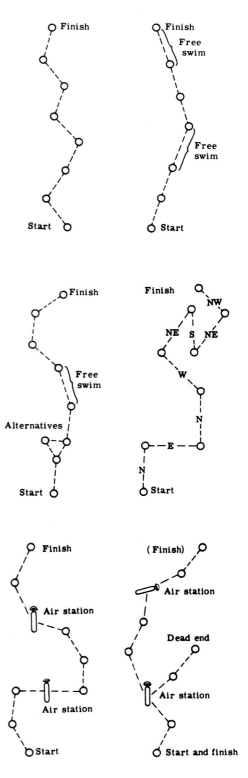

Fig. 67. Stepping stone courses.

CANDLES

The name comes from the shape of the apparatus which is something like a candelabrum. It is made from two pieces of wood each 1m in length joined at the centre in the form of a cross. There are four flotation chambers – one at each end of the cross. In the middle of the cross where the two pieces of wood join is a weight in the shape of a ball (an indoor athletic shot is ideal). The task is to bring the weight to the surface from the bottom of the pool, balanced on the cross. The technique is similar to that employed in 'Spiro' but there is a lot more finning involved and controlled breathing. The subject inverts his snorkel and blows air into each of the flotation chambers in any order he chooses but he must not touch the cross. It can be made more interesting (for the spectators!) if there is a small hole drilled in the top of each chamber. Now you will recognise how it got its name. See Fig. 68 for details.

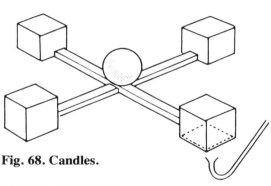

Fig. 68. Candles.

GROUP ACTIVITIES

Treasure Hunt

Everyone is required to take part in this activity as it uses the whole pool. Participants wear 'blacked-out' masks and fins and the hunt starts with them sitting round the pool edge listening to coins (2p) being thrown into the water. On a command everyone slides quietly into the pool and feels along the bottom collecting as many coins as possible. There are two possible ways of winning – 1, by collecting the most coins or 2, by having a coin with a particular date. Anyone who touches his mask *for any reason* on the surface is immediately disqualified. Clearing and adjustments must be completed underwater. The pool sides are 'out of bounds' after the start.

Those taking part in this activity are learning to dive by touch and cope with vertigo which will occur even in the pool situation after a time. It is surprising the number of different reasons given for removing the 'blacked-out' mask! There is also the close proximity of other divers and the possibility of collision which encourages participants to try and 'sense' each other and respond to the unexpected.

Pass the Parcel

A diver carrying his lung sits on the bottom of the pool. Twenty seconds later he is joined by another diver in basic gear and they share the lung. Twenty seconds later the two divers are joined at the bottom by a third and all three have to share the one lung. So the game progresses with the aim of having the maximum number of divers sharing one lung. The time is taken from the first diver submerging until any member of the group breaks surface. The divers are not required to share consecutively and can work out their own routine. It is not an activity for the inexperienced (remember compressed air is being used) and any number above nine can be considered good.

King Ball

A street game played by children – it adapts very well to the pool session. It is played by four or more wearing fins only and need not use the whole pool. One player is 'out' and is not allowed to wear fins but has a light plastic football to throw at the others. While on his own he may swim with the ball and the object is to hit any other player while they are on the surface. When this happens that player is 'out' and removes his fins. He can either take the place of the striker, who then puts on his fins, or join him as a team. In this case they are not allowed to swim with the ball. The numbers gradually build up until there is only one 'free' player left and he then becomes the striker and all the others go free with fins.

The skills of surface diving and underwater swimming receive a lot of practise in this activity but it also encourages participants to have much more awareness of surfacing techniques.

Blind Man

Another game from childhood for four or more players. The 'blind man' wears fins and a blacked-out mask. The remainder have mask and snorkel only. The blind man has the task of touching any other player above or below the surface and when he does so that player becomes the blind man in turn. A simple activity but it is quite effective in teaching buoyancy control and a quiet surface dive.

Relay Race

Teams are formed from two or more divers in basic gear and each one is required to swim two lengths (50m approximately) underwater. Each team has one aqualung which, in effect, forms the baton. The first member of each team holds the aqualung in his arms and jumps into the pool. They swim one length underwater and turn. After this turn the second member of the team may jump at any time he wishes and swim underwater to collect the lung in passing. Everything must be completed underwater and all entries and exits must be affected within 1m of the pool end. The winning team is the first one out of the water with all its members having swam two lengths underwater.

It is not an activity for the inexperienced but as the technique is acquired the length of the individual 'legs' can be increased. The race can also be run as a train similar to 'pass the parcel'. Instead of leaving the pool at the end of his two lengths the first diver is joined by the second and they share for the next two and are then joined by their third member and finally by a fourth!

Obstacle Course

In a 'follow-my-leader' manner the BTP take the lead through, round, under and over a variety of obstacles and the trainees have to copy the routine exactly. It can also be performed as 'chariots' with a fully kitted diver in blacked-out mask being steered from behind by a skindiver. The two are connected by a rope in each hand and use the normal signal code plus any others they care to add. Now try guiding the diver with a single line while standing on the pool side!

(Chapter 2 was written by Ron McIntyre.)

Chapter 3

Training lecture material

Up to this point we have concentrated on the practical abilities you must acquire in order to dive. Now we turn to the theory and facts you should master. Some of the facts have already been described but this chapter is set out as a series of lists of the contents that should be in each lecture. It should serve to let the trainee know what he or she should learn and to remind the lecturer of the contents required. Additional material should be added by the lecturer if he or she thinks fit.

In a sense this chapter completes the first part of the Training Manual which deals with the requirements for the training described in the Training Schedule. Later chapters provide much of the information you should receive in these lectures.

SNORKEL LECTURES

Training organisation

Explain purpose of training: safety of yourself and others, enjoyment, and development of your own self-training abilities. Outline tests as sequence from Snorkel to 3rd Class but do not detail tests. Explain further development of training to 2nd and 1st Class, Club Instructor and Examiner. Explain organisation of training in your branch and in the Club. Explain how trainees find somebody to train them, where and when, and who, how their training schedule is signed up, need to get signing up by BTP. Explain position of BTP, BDO and Branch Training Officer (if one). Explain any branch or pool authority rules about use of bath. Mention sources of information, e.g. diving manuals, branch and Club libraries.

Basic equipment and snorkel diving techniques

Purpose, best types and care of snorkel equipment. Explain best methods of surface finning. Surface signals demonstration. Duck diving and mask clearing. Dangers of hyperventilating (very simple at this stage). Air spaces in body – lungs, bronchi, trachea, buoyancy, Boyle's law very simply and effect of pressure on buoyancy.

Rescue, life saving and artificial respiration

Rescue involves a variety of situations (a) real or unnecessary panic, (b) threat of physical damage, (c) physical damage arising from outside factors, and (d) illness intrinsic to diver, e.g. onset of influenza, cramp etc.

Rescue requires (a) detection that diver is in trouble, (b) recovery to shore, (c) decision to cope with problem with local resources, e.g. very mild hypothermia treated by warm drinks, or to get expert help, doctor and/or ambulance, (d) recording details of what happened for future examination.

As a result (a) shore or boat watch or surface cover watches carefully particularly at points of greatest possible danger, (b) surface distress is noted and persons move by fastest route to victim, (c) *rescue methods in water* particularly approach, hold, releases if necessary, use of lifejackets or other buoyancy aids if available, (d) if unconscious or unresponsive EAR started as soon as possible (especially if hypoxic), (e) return to shore, first amateur diagnosis while on way, return by fastest route, (f) first aid or/and call of doctor or/and ambulance, (g) continued amateur treatment e.g. EAR as necessary until help arrives.

Practical demonstration of EAR and drill by audience.

Signals and surfacing drill

Purpose of signals. Surface signals: OK; Distress; Move in that direction; Stop. Underwater signals used by snorkeller, or which might require action by snorkeller: Underwater distress; Up; Down; Level off. Distress signals given by boats in trouble.

Surfacing drill. Cautious approach to surface.

Exhaustion, protective clothing, hypothermia

Symptoms and causes of exhaustion and hypothermia. Emphasise variability in reactions of different people to stress or cold. Recognising hypothermia. Treatment of exhaustion. Treatment of hypothermia and exhaustion. Types of protective clothing particularly wet suits and dry suits. Other methods of minimising risk of hypothermia, e.g. duration of immersion, warm drinks or warm water into suit. Emphasise dangers of chilling after the dive. 'Windchill' problem. Protective clothing, e.g. windproofs.

Ears and sinuses

Simple anatomy of air spaces in head, including eustachian tubes, inner, middle and outer parts of ear, ear drum, sinuses as dead ends. Blocking of these spaces by mucus and consequent effects of pressure, e.g. change of volume on change of pressure. Dangers of breaking ear drums, pushing infected mucus into middle ear or end of sinuses. Hence one of the reasons for not diving with a cold. Symptoms, especially dizziness on breaking ear drum, bleeding from sinus, nose or middle ear (through eustachian tubes). Methods of ear clearing, swallowing, palate and tongue method, blowing against nose, slow descent and ascent. Reversed ears.

Simple diagram of air spaces in head, either on blackboard or simple physiology charts, often borrowable from first aid classes, RLSS teachers or purchasable from Philip Harris Limited, Oldmixon, Weston-super-Mare.

Respiration, hypoxia, hyperventilation, drowning

Purpose of respiration is transport of oxygen to tissues and of carbon dioxide from tissues. Percentages of oxygen, nitrogen, CO_2 in inspired and expired air. Route of air from mouth or nose to lungs, including alveoli. Combination of oxygen with haemoglobin in red blood cells. Route of blood pumped by heart from lungs to heart, arteries, capillaries. Release to tissues. Route of carbon dioxide from tissues to capillaries, veins, heart, pulmonary artery to lungs.

Hypoxia, causes, i.e. obstruction to airway, hypoxic breathing gas, carbon monoxide poisoning. Symptoms, subjective and objective. Treatment.

Hyperventilation. Definition. Stimulus to breathe. Effect of hyperventilation on this. Danger in snorkel divers that it leads to hypoxia and death. Avoidance.

Drowning – three types:

a. hypoxia without water entering lungs, so-called blue drowning. Recognition and treatment;

b. water in lungs, when water is salt, so-called white drowning, hemoconcentration. Recognition and treatment;

c. freshwater in lungs, a form of white drowning. Very rapid death from hemodilution. Treatment if possible.

Explanation of physiological basis of EAR. Free supply of oxygenated air to lungs and removal of vitiated air.

(Use board, diagrams or charts, sources mentioned above.)

THIRD CLASS DIVER LECTURES

Effects of pressure

Boyle's Law. Units used in measurement of volume and pressure (please try and use metric units, either litres and bars, or, better cubic metres and newtons per m^2). Older members will prefer units such as cubic feet. Effects of pressure on air spaces, closed and open. Pressure at various depths of sea water.

Pressure and volume in aqualung cylinders. Thus consumption at various depths assuming constant rate of breathing. Effects of holding breath on ascent.

Dalton's law of partial pressures. Hence concentration of oxygen and nitrogen at various depths.

Henry's Law. Solubility of gases and pressure. Hence decompression sickness at very simple level.

Principles of the aqualung

Basic concept. A store of breathing air in cylinders under high pressure which is reduced to ambient pressure through the valves in the demand valve.

Cylinders. Definitions of working pressure, test pressure, test date and meaning of 'in test'. Steel and aluminium cylinders. Correct colour coding. Contents at various pressures. Pillar valve, balanced and unbalanced. Care and servicing of cylinders and valves. O-ring. Manifolds. Cylinder buoyancy.

Regulator. Basic idea of pressure sensing element controlling valve releasing high pressure air. Start explanation with a single stage regulator such as the Mistral, stripped in front of the class if possible. Use of diaphragms and pistons. Up-stream and downstream valves. Two stage regulators such as (a) Merlin, and (b) single hose regulators. Details of second stage regulator in single hose. Pressure in line between first and second stages. Pressure release valves in single hose regulators with downstream first stage. Care and maintenance of regulators. Disposal of exhaled air, valves involved in this. Visual aids should include sectional diagrams of regulators.

Aqualung use and buoyancy control

Assembling regulator onto aqualung. Testing regulator. Test contents pressure with contents gauge. Check air can be breathed from regulator. Turn off, watch contents gauge to see if pressure falls due to small leaks. Breathe out remaining air and check that the regulator does not deliver air through the exhalation route due to leaks. Turn on cylinder pillar valve again. Precautions to be used if no contents gauge is available. Adjusting harness. Correct position of harness with respect to lifejacket and weight belt. Proper length of harness straps and use of quick releases. (This can be done almost as a drill, maybe at pool side.)

Sources of bouyancy: degree of lung filling, variable buoyancy due to neoprene wet suits, use of ABLJs and/or dry suits as a source of buoyancy, advantages and disadvantages of direct feed or independent air bottle as a source of air for buoyancy, buoyancy by finning.

Judging neutral buoyancy. Go through sequence of dive, starting with pre-dive check, descent, signals, ascent, safe ascent rate, change back to snorkel, surface signals. Checking on amount of air remaining during the dive. Precautions if contents gauge not used.

Buoyancy control by weighting, finning, breath control, use of ABLJ and/or dry suit. Desirability of dry suit divers using suit for buoyancy control and ABLJ only for emergency situations. Awareness of problems of two sources of buoyancy. Dangers of being overweight.

Pulmonary barotrauma and emergency ascent

Cause of pulmonary barotrauma: excess pressure in all or part of air spaces in lung.

Types:
1. Air embolism. Definition. Symptoms. Treatment as far as it is possible. Emphasise that this condition can be contracted in ascents from as little as 3m depth and that it is very likely to be rapidly fatal. Risk of pulmonary bullae and colds. Need for X-ray examination.
2. Pneumothorax. Collapsed lung(s). Cause air in pleural cavity. Symptoms. Treatment.
3. Emphysema. Escape of air into tissue spaces, particularly under skin. Symptoms. Treatment. Mediastinal Emphysema.

Prevention. Do not dive unless you have had a chest X-ray and medical examination. Do not dive with a cold. Slow ascents, at a quarter of a metre a second. Breathing out during fast ascents and regularly in and out during normal ascents. Need to watch fellow diver and stop him if not breathing in and out.

Air endurance and air cylinders

Enlarge on contents of principles of aqualung lecture. Explain normal assumptions about breathing rate and thus dive planning, pointing out great risk that not enough air for decompression will be available unless deep dive well planned. Point out ways of controlling air consumption rate exist but are (a) not very reliable since cold, active finning or hard work will increase consumption, and (b) there may be risk of mild carbon dioxide poisoning at depth if breathing rate slow. However a warm, relaxed diver moving economically, gracefully and without apprehension, tends to have a low rate of air consumption. Emphasise need for good dive planning.

Air cylinders. Enlarge on contents of 'Principles of Aqualung' lecture. Mention British Standard Specifications. Cylinders should now conform to specifications of BS 5045 whether steel or aluminium alloy. HOS, HOT and HOA1 specifications now superseded but cylinders manufactured to them can be used. Maximum size of cylinder permitted under BS 5045 (120 cu.ft. at present). Note that cylinders in use in public domain, including roads in UK must conform to BS 5045. Rules about transport of filled cylinders by road and car insurance. Stamped marks on cylinders and their meaning. 'In-test' rules.

Dangers of using very negatively buoyant cylinders, e.g. lack of safety margin on dropping weight belt.

Importance of using air meeting BSI levels: air testing by and for branches.

Maintenance of equipment and diving accessories

Need to wash equipment, salt and grit. How to wash suit, demand valves, harness, lifejackets, outside of cylinders, compasses, etc. Ways of protecting equipment while in use, e.g. knee pads, wristlets covering watch, cylinder covers, taping and dangers of taping. Careful diving practice, i.e. careful well chosen entries and exits from water, not finning along bottom, not bumping into wrecks etc.

Maintenance (a) simple jobs that can be done at home, such as glueing and sewing-up wet suit repairs, cleaning inside of second stage valves, painting cylinders, (b) checking for repairs to be done by you, or professionally, at end of each dive. Need for annual servicing of regulators. Need to check that depth gauges, compasses etc. are still accurate. Use of compass, depth gauge, watch, torches, flashers, thermometer, etc. Points to notice in purchasing these.

Open water diving and dive procedure

The open water environment: waves, tides and currents, boats and the dangers they bring both in freshwater and seawater. Depth and low visibility dangers. How to find out about these before the dive.

Dangers of dive procedure: e.g. getting lost, becoming ill or apprehensive, equipment failure. Minimising these dangers and maximising safety procedures. Wrecks.

Waves: do not dive in seas above state 5 (state 3 if inexperienced). Entry and exit, boat and shore.

Tides and currents: dive at slack.

Boats and fairways. Use of diving flag. Dive out of fairways, surfacing procedure.

Deep diving, dangers especially of narcosis, decompression sickness, air exhaustion. Procedures. Use of decompression stops.

Low visibility diving: dangers. Use of buddy lines, lamps, and flashers. Psychological problems of low visibility diving.

Sudden illness in divers. Use of signals. Slow ascent if possible. Decompression or barotrauma risks. Use of lifejackets.

Equipment failure. Prevention by care and pre-dive check. Sharing, emergency ascent procedures.

Run through a typical dive. A. Briefing and actions of Dive Leader. B. Entry from shore or boat. C. Frequency of checks. D. Simple underwater navigation. E. Check on use of air. F. Reason for finishing dive. G. Surfacing. H. Coming ashore or entry to boat. I. Debrief and dive records.

Description and use of lifejackets

Main types of lifejacket.

SLJ: Construction; Fitting; Inflation and Deflation; Use. ABLJ: Construction; Fitting; Inflation and Deflation; Use.

Mention oral, bottle or direct feed inflation. ABLJ dangers and reference to training programme.

Buoyancy compensators. Construction. Fitting. Use.

Comparison of three types. Dangers of over-reliance on buoyancy aids.

Decompression (elementary treatment)

Simple description of the symptoms of decompression sickness, joint and muscle pain, paralysis, mental effects. Cause, bubbles in tissue due to release of nitrogen absorbed during dive. Responsibility and actions of expedition leader and others in event of real or suspected incident. Transport to recompression chamber. Concept of no-stop dive and importance of knowing durations for various depths. Definitions of 'no-stop', bottom time, ascent and descent rates. Use of RNPL tables in detail. What to do if you do not know your dive duration or suspect that you may be at risk. Point out that divers at the start of their diving career should not attempt dives that might lead to decompression requirements. Trainees before 3rd Class Award must not attempt decompression dives.

SECOND CLASS LECTURES

Safety and Emergency Procedure

Basically this lecture examines a number of standard emergency situations and how you should respond to them. For a start it should however be pointed out that a clear dive plan with a predetermined maximum depth, duration and ending point, good signals, observations of each other and of depth gauges, watches, contents gauges etc. and sensible appreciation of the constraints put upon the dive by currents, waves, water temperatures etc. is likely to prevent accident.

Emergencies.

a. Regulator failure or air exhaustion. If reasonably close, sharing, when rhythm established ascent to surface, if not close, ABLJ ascent (breathing from ABLJ).

b. Over-buoyant ascent, as on loss of weight belt. Breathe out as much as possible, fins at right angles to ascent or fin down, blow off any air in ABLJ. Grab partner.

c. Fainting or lack of response to signals. Partner rescues, removing weight belt if necessary or slightly inflating ABLJ, lift watching victim, replace mouthpiece if possible but above all prevent pulmonary barotrauma, either feet-first ascent or more likely neck straight, head up. EAR on surface.

d. Trapped diver. Partner assesses air supply remaining, possibility of releasing diver rapidly and without undue risk to him or herself. If air supply very short or release very difficult partner surfaces for help, maybe giving trapped diver his set, using ABLJ ascent. Standby diver and spare sets used in rescue.

e. Use of free ascent. Avoid if possible but technique if necessary.

f. Ascent following high pressure air escape. Note that though breathing may be possible air may blow off so fast that a normal ascent from any reasonable depth to the surface is not possible. Note that sharing is not possible unless victim fins laterally to keep out of bubble mass so that he or she can see demand valve. ABLJ ascent may be best.

Nitrogen absorption and narcosis

Factors affecting gas solubility: partial pressure, explain this concept carefully, temperature, nature of material, i.e. watery or fatty tissue. Also gas diffusibility. Uptake curves, showing saturation and half-saturation times. Importance of blood transport. Fast and slow saturating tissues. Also details of release of gas from the body on drop of partial pressure of nitrogen in the breathing gas, i.e. on ascending.

Nitrogen narcosis as a form of inert gas narcosis. Onset of symptoms as partial pressure approaches 4 ATA. Symptoms stressing variability. Dangers. Cure, ascent to level at which symptoms pass off.

Decompression

Remind audience of curves of uptake and release of absorbed dissolved gas. Introduce modern idea that supersaturation cannot occur but that silent bubbles form as soon as your body gets into a potential supersaturation condition. If potential partial pressure of gas dissolved exceeds partial pressure in breathing gas, bubbles form. If the excess is very marked the bubbles are large enough to produce symptoms. Symptoms from mildest to fatal ones. Recognition of symptoms and immediate first aid. Take to recompression chamber.

Use simple graphs to demonstrate principle of no-stop dives and why short dives lead to short decompression stops. Principles of decompression stops. Practical methods of carrying out stops. Use of decompression tables and calculation of decompression requirements.

Very simple outline of basis of therapeutic decompression. Repetitive dives. Decompression meters. Diving at altitude. Flying after diving.

Oxygen poisoning, carbon dioxide and carbon monoxide poisoning

Oxygen poisoning. Cause, O_2 pp. exceeding 1.75 ATA. Symptoms, tunnel vision, twitching, pallor, followed by unconsciousness and convulsions. Particular danger of convulsions. Treatment, reduce O_2 partial pressure.

Carbon dioxide poisoning. Cause CO_2 partial pressure raised above normal in inhaled breathing gas, due to air contamination, dead space etc. Mild symptoms, apprehension, increased respiration rate. Panic, nausea, flushed skin. Unconsciousness. Treatment, restore supply of air free of CO_2 or nearly so.

Carbon monoxide poisoning. Cause, contaminated air from both internal combustion engine and electrical compressors. Symptoms, headaches, tunnel vision, unconsciousness, death. Lack of symptoms at depth. Treatment, access to fresh air or oxygen.

Underwater navigation and search methods

Methods:

1. Use of compass, with practical work.
2. Ripple markings and sunlight underwater.
3. Underwater topography and depths after study of chart.

4. Underwater lines, lights etc.

Search methods, judged by area to be searched, type of bottom and size of object sought. Circular sweeps, jack-stay snag line, swim line searches.

Basic seamanship

Start by emphasising that seamanship is above all a practical attainment and that practice in use of a boat is essential. However the following theoretical aspects should be known to the diver. Types of boat, good and bad points.

Outline types of manoeuvre, launch, under way, anchoring, beaching, recovery of boat.

Understanding of tides, use of tide tables. Use of pilot books, almanacs and tide tables to work out rate, time and direction of currents.

Simple weather forecasting.

Signals used by other boats and shore establishments.

Buoys (IALA system).

Rules of road and courteous behaviour by small boats used by divers.

Expedition organisation

(See in detail Chapter 9)

Pre-planning and organisation. Appointment and duties of officers.

Assessment of site, for dangers and procedures.

Dive plan. Communication of this to divers etc.

Emergency and rescue precautions.

Logging the expedition, during and afterwards.

Debrief and departure from site.
Further actions.

Compressor operation

Physics of air compression. Basic features of the construction of a compressor. Stages. Interstage cooling. Mechanical de-watering and de-oiling. Use of 'drain' or 'blow-down' valves. Filtering. Main points of practical operation. Air purity standards. Testing air. Legal aspects relating to cylinders.

Further actions

Knowledge of lecture material is tested by oral or written examination for Snorkel Diver and 3rd Class certificates. The choice of oral or written examination is at the discretion of the BDO or BTO. Examination of your knowledge of 2nd Class lecture material is by questions requiring written answers so that the Club has clear evidence that you possess a level of theoretical knowledge appropriate for the award and for the Instructor and other Club courses that are open to you when you have obtained the 2nd Class certificate. Multiple choice examination formats are recommended for written examinations.

Attendance at lectures arranged by your branch is strongly recommended but if you find this difficult the BDO should sign you as passed for the appropriate certificate provided you pass the test on lecture material and, of course, pool or open water tests.

Chapter 4

Basic Physiology for Divers

The physiological properties of your body determine how you can dive. As a consequence, an understanding of physiology allows you to realise which diving practices are likely to be reasonably safe, which rather hazardous, which very hazardous and which deadly. In addition, a simple knowledge of physiology will allow you to make a more informed attempt at first-aid should an accident occur.

This chapter is divided into three sections: (A) a short, mainly pictorial description of the parts of the body and the normal processes that go on in them; (B) a description of each type of physiological disorder associated with diving in a standard format and (C) ear clearing techniques.

A. NORMAL HUMAN PHYSIOLOGY FOR DIVERS

1. The absolute pressure increases steadily with increasing water depth at a rate of 1 bar per 10 metres, so that the absolute pressure at a depth x metre is given by $\frac{x}{10} + 1$ bar. (The 1 bar is added because of the pressure of the air at the surface of the water.) (In SI units pressure is measured in Newtons per square metre: 1 bar = 100,000 Newtons per square metre.) 1 Bar is equivalent to 760mm of Mercury (Hg). The **partial pressure** of a gas in a mixture, e.g. oxygen in air, is the pressure that the particular gas exerts, in other words the total pressure × the proportion of that gas in the mixture. Thus at 40m of seawater the total pressure of seawater is 5 bar. Since air is ⁴/₅ nitrogen, the partial pressure of nitrogen in air at 5 bar is ⁴/₅ × 5 bar = 4 bar or 3040mm Hg.

2. Water and body tissues are nearly incompressible, but the air or gas in the spaces in the body are compressible, see Figs. 69 and 70.

3. Any air space in the body which is closed off from connection with a breathing air (gas) supply at ambient pressure will be compressed as a diver descends and will tend to become smaller. In a snorkel diver breathholding, this will mean all gas spaces. In an aqualung diver taking in a supply of air at the same pressure as the surrounding sea at his depth, it will mean only those air spaces that have remained closed off from his supply of air as he descends. All the other air spaces will have had their pressure brought up to that of the surrounding body and sea by the inflow of gas from the breathing supply. The volumes of the closed off air spaces will expand during ascent.

4. Closed off air or gas spaces in the body will not be harmed by compression if they are entirely surrounded by soft tissues, e.g. gas spaces in the gut. Most closed off air spaces can usually be opened temporarily by a diver to allow the pressure to equalise with the ambient pressure, e.g. middle ear.

5. If the closed off air spaces are partly surrounded by hard bony tissue, there will be some resistance to compression and collapse of the air space as the diver descends. At some point mechanical collapse of some part of the wall of the air space will occur with injury to the local tissues, e.g. cavities in your teeth.

For instance:
In both snorkel and aqualung divers, the following closed off air spaces may be found which can collapse, if not periodically opened by the diver, with the following effects, see Figs. 69 and 70.
There seems to be little evidence that any case of rib collapse has ever been seen because the depth at which it is likely to occur is in excess of most, perhaps all, snorkel dives yet made. Incidentally, snorkel divers become less buoyant with increasing depth because of lung compression, see Fig. 71, and blood and gut cavity organs are pushed up into the rib cage.

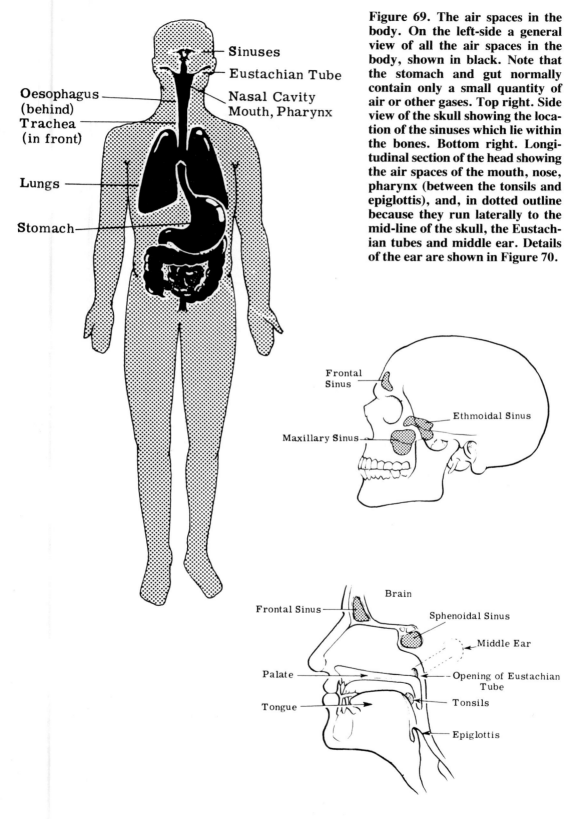

Figure 69. The air spaces in the body. On the left-side a general view of all the air spaces in the body, shown in black. Note that the stomach and gut normally contain only a small quantity of air or other gases. Top right. Side view of the skull showing the location of the sinuses which lie within the bones. Bottom right. Longitudinal section of the head showing the air spaces of the mouth, nose, pharynx (between the tonsils and epiglottis), and, in dotted outline because they run laterally to the mid-line of the skull, the Eustachian tubes and middle ear. Details of the ear are shown in Figure 70.

Sinuses

Eustachian Tube

Nasal Cavity
Mouth, Pharynx

Oesophagus
(behind)
Trachea
(in front)

Lungs

Stomach

Frontal
Sinus

Ethmoidal Sinus

Maxillary Sinus

Brain

Frontal Sinus

Sphenoidal Sinus

Middle Ear

Palate

Opening of Eustachian
Tube

Tongue

Tonsils

Epiglottis

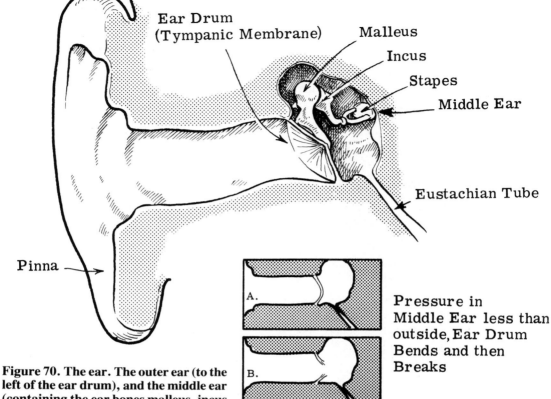

Ear Drum (Tympanic Membrane)

Malleus

Incus

Stapes

Middle Ear

Eustachian Tube

Pinna

Pressure in Middle Ear less than outside, Ear Drum Bends and then Breaks

Reversed Ear

Figure 70. The ear. The outer ear (to the left of the ear drum), and the middle ear (containing the ear bones malleus, incus and stapes) and Eustachian tube are shown. The inner ear which is a nerve structure is not shown in this diagram. The three insets A, B and C refer to effects of pressure differential on the ear drum leading A and B to Aural Barotrauma and C, to 'Reversed Ears'.

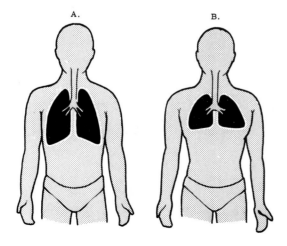

Figure 71. The relative sizes of the lungs (black) in a snorkel diver at A. the surface and B.10 metres depth. Note also how the waist line has changed on snorkel diving to 10m. Part of the space occupied formerly by the lungs now contains gut and blood contents, hence the snorkel diver has a slimmer waistline at depth. The reduction in volume of the lungs means that the snorkel diver loses buoyancy as he or she descends.

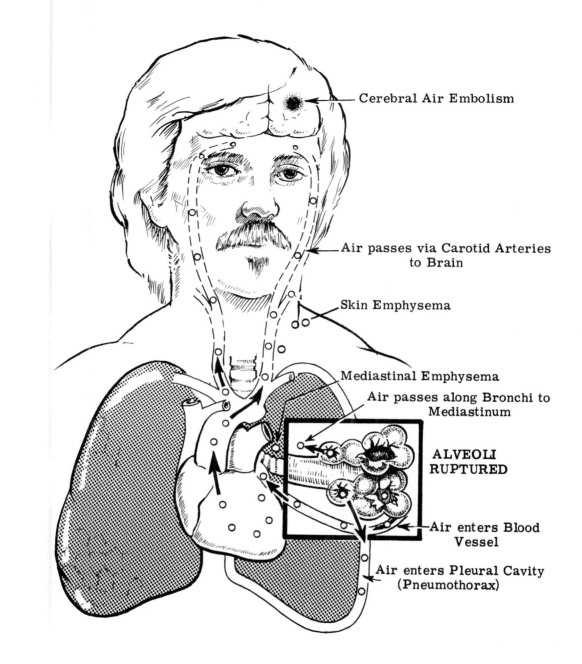

Cerebral Air Embolism

Air passes via Carotid Arteries to Brain

Skin Emphysema

Mediastinal Emphysema

Air passes along Bronchi to Mediastinum

ALVEOLI RUPTURED

Air enters Blood Vessel

Air enters Pleural Cavity (Pneumothorax)

Figure 72. Diagram to illustrate the causes of the four types of Pulmonary Barotrauma (Burst lung). If an aqualung diver ascends while holding his or her breath the air in the lung alveoli retains most or all of the pressure that it had when the diver last breathed. But the pressure of the water and thus on the rest of the body falls as the diver ascends. In consequence a pressure differential develops across the alveolar wall; when this is sufficient the alveoli rupture and air enters either the circulation (leading to an air embolism), or the lung lining (leading to pneumothorax) or tracks into the Mediastinum around the heart or lungs up to positions under the skin (leading to Mediastinal or Skin (Cutaneous) Emphysema).

TYPES OF DESCENT BAROTRAUMA

Space	Injured area	Name of injury
Middle ear	Ear drum or/and Eustachian tube	AURAL BAROTRAUMA
Sinuses	Sinus wall	SINUS BAROTRAUMA

Additionally snorkel divers may suffer, at least in theory, from the following injuries during descent because they cannot make up the volume of air spaces with gas from breathing equipment.

Lungs	Ribs	—

6. During descent, the snorkel or aqualung diver will attempt to let air into the closed air spaces of the ear and sinuses and will normally abandon the descent if he cannot do this, see EAR-CLEARING TECHNIQUES.

7. During ASCENT the snorkel diver is not at risk normally because air spaces are returning towards their normal size as air within them expands. However, air which has been transferred from lungs etc. to middle ear cavity during ear clearing adds to the expanding volume in this cavity so that, if this cannot escape through the Eustachian tube, the 'REVERSED EARS' syndrome may result. Wearing of tight hoods or ear plugs may cause 'reversed ears' during descent because air between the hood or plug and the ear drum will be at surface pressure while that in the middle ear will be at higher pressure, see Fig. 70.

8. During ascent, the aqualung diver is at considerable risk from the effects of expanding air (see Fig. 72) because of the additional mass of air in his body spaces taken up from breathing equipment while submerged. Unfortunately the diver can close off his or her epiglottis (see Fig. 69) so that air does not escape from the lungs, consequently the aqualung diver must breathe normally during ascent to prevent this. In addition, the middle ear, sinuses and occasionally the intestine, contain gas that will expand, may fail to escape and give pain.

9. Respiration consists basically of the transport of oxygen to the tissues and the elimination of carbon dioxide from the tissues. The diagram in Fig. 73 shows the route of transport of oxygen and of carbon dioxide, CO_2.

The oxygen route can be summarised as follows:

Air or oxygen in breathing mixture — nose or mouth — air passage to glottis — trachea — bronchi — bronchioles — alveoli (then it is dissolved and passes through alveolar and capillary walls and combines with haemoglobin in blood cells) — red blood cells then travel by capillaries to pulmonary vein — left auricle of heart — left ventricle — aorta — arteries — capillaries where it leaves the haemoglobin and passes in solution to the surrounding tissues.

The carbon dioxide route is:

Carbon dioxide leaves the tissues in solution and combines with other components of the red cell or travels in solution in the plasma starting in the capillaries and thence to venules — veins — vena cava — right auricle of the heart — right ventricle — pulmonary artery — thence through alveolar capillaries — alveolar wall in gaseous form to bronchioles — bronchi

TYPES OF ASCENT BAROTRAUMA

Space	Injured area	Name of injury
Middle ear	Ear drum or Eustachian tubes	REVERSED EARS or ASCENT AURAL BAROTRAUMA
Sinuses	Sinus wall	SINUS BAROTRAUMA OF ASCENT (usually painless)
Lungs	Lung and surrounding tissues, circulatory	PULMONARY BAROTRAUMA (EMPHYSEMA PNEUMOTHORAX and GAS EMBOLISM)
Teeth cavities	Tooth	DENTAL BAROTRAUMA
Intestine	Intestinal tissues	GASTROINTESTINAL BAROTRAUMA

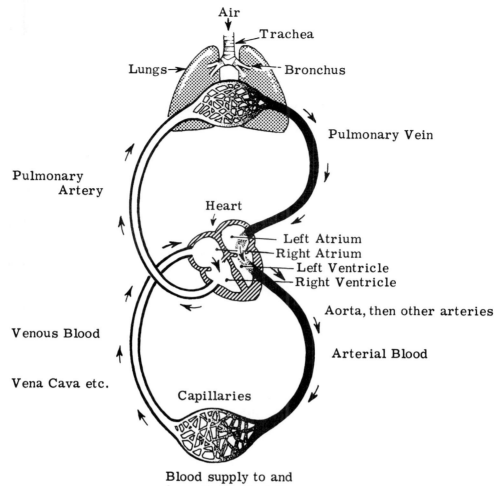

Air
Trachea
Lungs
Bronchus
Pulmonary Vein
Pulmonary Artery
Heart
Left Atrium
Right Atrium
Left Ventricle
Right Ventricle
Aorta, then other arteries
Venous Blood
Arterial Blood
Vena Cava etc.
Capillaries

Blood supply to and from the rest of the Body

Figure 73. The routes of oxygen (black) transport through the blood from the lung via the heart (left side) to the tissue capillaries and of carbon dioxide transport back from the capillaries via the heart (right side) to the lungs.

— trachea — glottis, and out by nose or mouth.

The expired air contains about 4% CO_2 so that if an appreciable amount of the expired air is rebreathed, the carbon dioxide intake will reach levels at which symptoms of carbon poisoning may result.

10. If insufficient oxygen is transported to the tissues, the body may develop HYPOXIA, lack of oxygen in the tissues. This is found in several types of injury. Hypoxia victims are often unconscious. The blood is purple (blue) so that the nail bed, the lips, the inside of the eyelids, the ear lobes are blue. Respiration may be weak or absent.

If insufficient carbon dioxide is transported away from the tissues, the body develops carbon dioxide poisoning or HYPERCAPNIA. In very heavy breathing at rest, too much carbon dioxide is removed from the tissues with a resulting condition called HYPOCAPNIA. Since the stimulus to breathe is controlled by the level of carbon dioxide in the body, hypocapnia may allow breathholding divers to faint from hypoxia before the desire to breathe is felt. This is the physiological reason for the danger of HYPERVENTILATION before snorkel diving. Hyperventilation is rapid deep breathing which provides more respired volume of air than is required by the body.

If too much oxygen is transported to the tissues, OXYGEN POISONING may result. The cause will always be a raised partial pressure of O₂ in the breathing air. The normal pressure of oxygen in air is 20% of 760, i.e. 152mm Hg. If you breathe pure oxygen at 1 bar total pressure, the partial pressure is 760mm. At 2 bar, if you breathe pure oxygen, the p.p. is 1520mm, a level which will cause clear oxygen poisoning.

11. The two main gases in air dissolve in the tissue and body fluids with oxygen being chemically bound by haemoglobin in the red cells. The amount dissolved (not in combination) is proportional to the partial pressure of that gas in the breathing mixture. Incidentally, at 30m depth, the partial pressure of oxygen in air is sufficient to dissolve an appreciable amount of oxygen in the fluid between the red cells, the plasma, as well as that carried by the haemoglobin in the red cells.

12. Nitrogen and other inert gases dissolved in the body fluids will at some partial pressure, cause the onset of INERT GAS NARCOSIS due to the derangement of nerve cell structure by the dissolved gas. This condition rapidly disappears if the partial pressure of these gases falls, as on ascent, below the onset value. Nitrogen narcosis is the only type the amateur diver is likely to experience.

13. During a dive there will be an uptake of dissolved nitrogen and some oxygen from the breathing air because of the increased partial pressure of these gases. Once the diver ascends towards the surface, this dissolved nitrogen will at some depth be in excess of the amount that could be dissolved under those conditions, so that it will be eliminated, partly through the lungs and partly by the formation of initially very small bubbles in the tissues. If these bubbles reach a certain size, they damage the tissues and cause DECOMPRESSION SICKNESS, often termed the 'bends'. Strictly speaking the 'bends' refers to decompression sickness of the joints and musculature. If the bubbles form in the nerves, permanent paralysis may result; if bubbles press on nerves, temporary paralysis may be caused. Usually, perhaps always, there is no problem with the oxygen because it is so rapidly consumed by the body that it is never found in excess concentration.

14. Diving often leads to the human body being cooled overmuch and this produces the condition called HYPOTHERMIA. (see below)

B. SYMPTOMS AND CAUSES OF PHYSIOLOGICAL DISORDERS CAUSED BY DIVING

1. Injury due to Expanding Gas. (See Fig. 72) Pulmonary Barotrauma (Burst Lung). 4 types.

(a) Gas Embolism (Air Embolism)

This form of embolism should be distinguished from embolism due to emboli of fat or cells which have no connection with diving. An embolus is a small body which tends to block the finer blood vessels.

Cause: Ascent with breathing passages blocked, as with breathholding. Some forms of equipment, in particular closed circuit equipment, can cause gas embolism if the pressure release valve jams during an ascent. Outset of symptoms is usually but not invariably rapid, during or after ascent. Also due to airway collapse in lungs during ascent which is likely to happen if diver has the condition of having pulmonary bullae, i.e. small pockets of air with very small or no openings to rest of lungs. Gas escapes from lungs into circulation.

Subjective symptoms: (i.e. those victim is aware of) Interference with senses, hallucinations, tunnel vision, loss of sensation, paralysis, visual and speech defects, pins and needles sensations.

Objective symptoms: (i.e. those detected by observers) Slight discharge of blood in mucus in mouth (but note that this can easily be confused with slight sinus bleeding or even middle ear bleeding which are symptoms of much less serious conditions), collapse, behavioural abnormalities, epileptic fit, sudden death. Free flowing regulators if firmly sealed in the mouth have been known to cause air embolism.

Treatment: If a recompression chamber is at hand, immediate recompression. Otherwise administer such first aid as will prevent further collapse and transport to doctor as soon as possible.

Situations in which air embolism may be found: An ascent during which the diver held breath. Very fast ascents (2 metres per second or faster) even if diver appears to breathe out. Faulty closed or semi-closed circuit equipment. Diving with any degree of bronchial inflammation, as in a cold, may increase risk of air embolism developing even in ascents during which correct rate of ascent and exhalation was used.

(b) Pneumothorax

Cause: Basic cause as with gas embolism, but gas escapes not into circulation but into the pleural cavity surrounding each lung causing lung collapse. It is unusual for both lungs to be affected but if they are, death from hypoxia results very rapidly.

Subjective symptoms: Pain in rib cage region, difficulty with breathing and swallowing.

Objective symptoms: As hypoxia, though if one lung is in good condition, the hypoxic symptoms will not be very marked.

Treatment: The victim must be given complete rest and medical help obtained to remove air from pleural cavity. EAR if breathing stops.

Situations in which it is likely to occur: As with gas embolism.

(c) Emphysema

Cause: Gas expands breaking alveoli and then tracking between tissues to either mediastinum, space between lungs around heart, or into neck (usually under skin – subcutaneous).

Two main types of Emphysema.
(a) Subcutaneous emphysema
(b) Mediastinal emphysema

Subjective symptoms:
(a) Subcutaneous – pain in skin region over chest and nearby skin areas.
(b) Mediastinal – possible difficulty with breathing or heart rhythm.

Objective symptoms:
(a) Subcutaneous – blueness of skin, local swellings. Skin has taut texture.
(b) Mediastinal – slight to serious effects on heart action.

Treatment: In the absence of less serious symptoms, little need be done for subcutaneous emphysema, though a doctor can remove the air. Otherwise take victim to hospital.

Situations in which it is likely to occur: As with gas embolism.

(d) Pulmonary Tissue Damage

Cause: Rupture of a few alveoli.

Symptoms: Breathing difficulties, cough, bloody sputum. This type of damage always precedes, a, b or c, and is not in itself too serious.

Situations in which it is likely to occur: As with gas embolism.

II. Injury due to either Expanding or Contracting Gas

1. Aural Barotrauma

Cause: Failure to open Eustachian tube between middle ear and throat during a descent or ascent, leads to a pressure differential existing between the middle ear cavity and its surroundings. As a consequence the ear drum tends to be pushed outwards (ascent) or inwards (descent) with risk of breaking it. If the Eustachian tube is filled with mucus, this may in a descent be carried into the middle ear with risk of infection. See Fig. 70.

Subjective symptoms: Range from slight to acute pain from middle ear region. If the ear drum ruptures, sudden extra pain and possible dizziness from entry of cold water into middle ear.

Objective symptoms: Range from slight inflammation to rupture of ear drum (these of course can only be determined after the dive). Bleeding from middle ear, usually routed down to Eustachian tube but through drum if broken. Note that barotrauma during ascent (reversed ears) is much rarer than that during descent and also that once a moderate negative pressure is established in the middle ear during descent, the Eustachian tube tends to 'lock' shut.

Treatment: The diver is usually very well aware of this form of injury and will endeavour to control his descent and ascent so that the effects are minimised. If the pain is marked, the diver must ascend (while on a descent) or descend (while on an ascent) to a point at which pain vanishes then after a short pause try continuing in intended direction slowly clearing ears frequently. If very severe on descent, abandon dive. If very serious on ascent, repeat relief procedure outlined in above and try and surface very slowly. If however onset of decompression problems and/or lack of breathing gas masks ascent imperative, do so. If eardrum ruptures, or is painful for more than a short time after reaching surface, or if any bleeding, seek medical help.

For prevention, see Ear clearing techniques.

Situations where it is likely to occur: Any ascent or descent particularly if diving with or after a cold.

2. Sinus Barotrauma (Sinus squeeze)

Cause: Pressure differential between sinus spaces and surrounding tissue. As a result, capillaries break and mucus cells discharge mucus into sinuses.

Objective symptoms: Slight bleeding from nose. Inflammation in sinus lining.

Subjective symptoms: Pain in facial region. In practice this is only likely during descent sinus barotrauma. Headache.

Treatment: The diver should not dive again until sinuses clear.

Situations in which it is likely to occur: As with aural barotrauma.

III. Partial Pressure Effects

1. Abnormal Partial Pressures of Oxygen

Note that the partial pressure of oxygen in the breathing mixture should not normally fall below 150mm Hg or rise above 1520mm (2 bar absolute), outside this range the partial pressures are abnormal. If air is used as the breathing mixture, there is no problem at all down to 90m plus.

(a) Oxygen Poisoning

Cause: Partial pressure of oxygen in breathing mixture above 2.0 bar. The greater the value of partial pressure above 2.0 bar, the more rapid the onset of symptoms, but there is much variability in rapidity of response from one person to another.

Subjective symptoms: Apprehension followed by disturbance to vision and auditory senses. Facial muscle twitching. At this point the victim usually becomes rapidly unconscious.

Objective symptoms: Pallor caused by constriction of narrow capillaries under skin. Twitching of muscles, loss of muscle control of legs and arms. Unconsciousness, convulsions. The victim usually holds breath for about 1 minute in the first stage of the convulsion but this does not give trouble, unless diver accidentally or deliberately ascends during this.

Treatment: Reduce partial pressure of oxygen to 0.2 bar, i.e. sea level air. EAR if necessary.

Situations in which oxygen poisoning may be found: Using pure oxygen rebreather at depths greater than 10m. Decompression on pure oxygen at such depths (unlikely).

(b) Hypoxia

Cause: Reduction of partial pressure oxygen in breathing mixture below 0.14 bar absolute.

Subjective symptoms: With moderate hypoxia a variety of nervous symptoms are possible but when severe, vision greys and becomes tunnel-like. Sounds seem indistinct and remote, dizziness, feeling of detachment. Note that the victim usually becomes unconscious before being really aware of them.

Objective symptoms: Cyanosed (blue) lips and fingernails and ear lobes. Skin pallor in other regions. Facial and vocal muscle control is lost. Breathing rate rises as does pulse rate. Unconsciousness and eventually death if oxygen partial pressure below 0.10 bar. The lower the value of the oxygen partial pressure below 0.10 bar, the more rapid the onset of unconsciousness and death. Death will normally follow when there is no oxygen in the breathing air within 8 minutes of unconsciousness. Note that death from drowning when no water enters the lungs is a death from lack of oxygen.

Treatment: Restore a supply of breathing gas containing at least 0.16 bar absolute (ATA) of oxygen to the victim. Artificial respiration and heart massage may be needed.

Situations in which hypoxia may be found: Breathholding after hyperventilation, aqualung cylinder filled with inert gas, drowning if glottal spasm (Laryngospasm) prevents water entering lungs. (For other type of drowning see V and for further details on this type also see V.)

2. Abnormal Partial Pressures of Carbon Dioxide

(a) Hypercapnia (Carbon dioxide poisoning)

Cause: Partial pressure of CO_2 in inspired breathing mixture above 0.03 bar. Remember that CO_2 level in normal air is 0.0003 bar at sea level pressure. Slight to moderate effects appear when the partial pressure rises to 0.01 bar and at 0.03 bar the diver will usually notice the effects and certainly so if not at rest. At 0.05 bar partial pressure, the effects are serious and at 0.1 bar, the diver will rapidly become unconscious followed by death at slightly higher levels.

Subjective symptoms: At first occasional apprehension developing into a general anxiety. Since diving induces apprehension in many people to a slight degree, the diver may usually fail to realise the cause at this stage. Breathlessness develops into panting and simultaneously almost uncontrollable panic appear. The extent of these symptoms and the rapidity with which they develop increases as the partial pressure rises. The victim will often be sick or feel as though he or she wishes to vomit.

Afterwards there will invariably be a headache.

Objective symptoms: Breathing rate rises, initially with deep breathing. This will develop into intense panting which is less effective in ventilating the lungs followed by shallow breathing as the victim becomes unconscious. The pulse rate rises as the panting develops but drops at the onset of unconsciousness. The skin, particularly in the face, is flushed due to vasco-dilation (swelling of blood vessels). The victim may act irrationally in attempts to get more air to breathe. Unconsciousness, muscular rigidity, followed by death at high levels of the gas.

Treatment: Reduce the partial pressure of CO_2 in the breathing mixture to below 0.01 bar. EAR if necessary.

Situations in which CO_2 poisoning may be found: Contaminated supply of breathing gas. Use of badly designed breathing equipment, especially when very hard work is attempted in such equipment at depth.

(b) Hypocapnia (Danger due to hyperventilation)

Cause: Hyperventilation washes CO_2 out of blood. Since desire to breathe is controlled by CO_2 level in the blood, breathholding ability is lengthened in people who have hyperventilated. As a consequence, a snorkel diver who hyperventilates becomes hypocapnic and thus can become hypoxic and unconscious before he wishes to breathe.

Symptoms: In cases of prolonged hyperventilation before breathholding, dizziness, tingling, headache, nausea. In snorkel diving after hyperventilation, the effects of hypoxia may be seen.

Treatment: Stop anyone hyperventilating. If unconscious during a snorkel dive, treat for drowning after bringing them to surface.

Situations where hypocapnia may occur: Untrained and ill-advised snorkel diver.

3. Carbon Monoxide Poisoning

Cause: Carbon monoxide contamination of breathing gas. Effect is dependent on partial pressure so that 40 pp million while having almost no effect at 1 bar will have a marked effect at 5 bar. Extent of poisoning also depends on duration of exposure.

Subjective symptoms: Note that symptoms are hardly expressed at depths of 30m or more, and that the symptoms do not develop until the diver surfaces or moves into shallow water. Headache. Feeling of weakness. Visual disturbance. Nausea.

Objective symptoms: Cherry red colour to blood, noticeable in lips. Confused behaviour. Vomiting. Unconsciousness. Death.

Treatment: Restore a supply of carbon monoxide free air or other breathing gas to the diver.

Conditions in which carbon monoxide poisoning might occur: Inadequate precautions to keep breathing gas pure and with carbon monoxide level above permitted limit.

4. Inert Gas Narcosis

Cause: Inert gas partial pressure in excess of following values:

NITROGEN 4.0 BAR

NEON 50 BAR (this figure is provisional)

HELIUM 55 BAR (this figure is provisional)

For the amateur diver, only nitrogen need be considered. It should be noted that these onset values are only approximate and different individuals on different occasions show variable values at which effects start. Effects become rapidly more serious as the partial pressure rises above these onset values.

Subjective symptoms: Intoxication similar in many ways to alcoholic intoxication, and thus the victim may not be aware or may be able to pretend subsequently that he or she was not aware of the symptoms. Judgement deteriorates. The first symptom detectable by an observant victim is a loss in visual acuity so that objects appear less sharp and appear as though seen through dirtier water. The onset of narcosis is extremely rapid so that the victim is not aware of the symptoms developing so long as he or she remains at a constant high level of inert gas partial pressure.

Objective symptoms: Intoxication is observed in the victim, initially control of fine movements, problem solving and dexterity decrease. With higher partial pressures of the gas, the victim carries out irrational actions, loses fine control of movement and eventually becomes unconscious. At any point in this sequence, death by drowning may intervene.

Treatment: Reduce the partial pressure of inert gas, usually by reducing the diving depth by ascent until the symptoms disappear.

Situations in which inert gas narcosis appears: Deep diving, i.e. beyond 40 metres using air. At 50m, most divers are lightly narcosed, a few heavily so, by 60m symptoms are clear and hazardous to most divers.

IV. Partial Pressure Effects With Gas Expansion

1. Decompression Sickness (Also known as Bends, Caisson disease)

Cause: When partial pressure of any inert gases, e.g. nitrogen, in tissues appreciably exceeds partial pressure of that inert gas in breathing mixture. In practice for diving on air the diver is at risk if the partial pressure of nitrogen in the tissues exceeds 1.6 times that in breathing mixture, whether this is at surface or at depth during the ascent. Thus symptoms only develop on or subsequent to (more typically) ascents which are rapid enough after sufficient bottom time by the diver and from sufficient depths to permit the condition stated above to apply. Bottom time is duration from leaving the surface till start of ascent at 15m per minute or till ascending to 9m depth if ascent rate is incorrect. If the ascent is too slow the diver will pick up an appreciably larger loading of nitrogen than he or she would have had if they had ascended at the correct rate. This is the reason for the alternate definitio of bottom time as 'or until the 9 metre depth' has been passed during ascent. Ascent at the correct rate allows you to eliminate a small amount of nitrogen during the ascent. Tables for these rates of ascent are known as Decompression tables and use 'stops' rather than a continuous slow ascent. (For fuller explanation see Introductory Manual).

Subjective symptoms: (Arranged in order of increasing severity) Undue tiredness (not an important or diagnostic symptom), itching skin, pain in joints or muscles. Pain in chest (possibly indicative of imminent difficulty in breathing). Pins and needles in limbs. Paralysis. Defective vision.

Objective symptoms: Complaint of pain as above. Skin mottling in some cases. Difficulty in breathing. Paralysis. Shock varying in severity from case to case. In severe cases, rapid death often from heart failure and/or loss of breathing. Note that the symptoms vary very much from case to case, and that they tend to increase in severity for up to 24 hours after the initial accident; indeed no symptoms may be noticeable for 10 minutes to several hours after the accident. It should also be noted that though symptoms tend to be more severe if the inert gas partial pressure excess was greater rather than slight, there is a great deal of variation from individual to individual and from occasion to occasion so that occasionally divers who are only slightly at risk produce more serious symptoms than those who are more at risk. Note also that symptoms are in many ways similar to those of gas embolism and to those of various cardiovascular and nervous diseases. The person controlling diving at the time should know whether each diver is likely to be at risk from decompression sickness and this and the rapidity of onset of the symptoms should allow a diagnosis between decompression sickness and gas embolism.

Treatment: Immediate recompression in a chamber, but medical help must be obtained as soon as possible. Before medical help arrives, the victim must be accompanied and first-aid given, if necessary, particularly for shock, and EAR if necessary. Open water therapeutic recompression is not to be attempted unless it is quite clear that transport to a recompression chamber cannot be achieved within 12 hours and then only if adequate air supplies available. In other words, if the accident occurs anywhere in UK, most of Europe and many other areas, open water therapeutic recompression is not to be attempted. If the diver is known to be at risk but has not developed any symptoms, open water recompression should be attempted using RNPL tables.

Situations in which there is a risk of decompression sickness: Badly planned or executed dives in 16m or more depth. Inadequate briefing of divers, inadequate equipment used by divers, repetitive diving. Rescue diving may present a particular hazard because in such situations there is a strong tendency for good planning and supervision to collapse in the natural wish to do all that is possible to help.

Physical basis of decompression. The amount of gas dissolved in fluid, and for these purposes we can regard the human body as a fluid, is proportional to the partial pressure of that gas in the gas phase in contact with the fluid. But if the partial pressure of a gas in the breathing mixture is changed, it takes an appreciable time for the partial pressure of dissolved gas to adjust completely to the change.

As a consequence, if a diver, breathing air, makes even only a short shallow descent, the increased partial pressure of nitrogen in the air he is breathing causes the partial pressure of nitrogen dissolved in his body to rise. When he ascends, at some point before he reaches the surface, the partial pressure of nitrogen dissolved in him will exceed the partial pressure of nitrogen in his lungs. At this point, the excess partial pressure of dissolved nitrogen will be relieved by the gas coming out of the solution in his tissues as minute bubbles. If the partial pressure excess is slight, the bubbles are so small that they have no effect; in this case, they are known as silent bubbles. However, if the excess is appreciable because the dive was deeper and/or longer so that more inert gas was dissolved, the bubbles will be larger, large enough to produce symptoms. The larger and more numerous the large bubbles, the more serious are the symptoms.

The above is the modern theory of decompression sickness. Note that it is very different from the supersaturation theory formerly proposed. That theory allowed there to be a certain degree of supersaturation before bubbles would form. This is true of very clean fluids but ones full of small particles (i.e. nucleation centres) cannot be supersaturated. The body is full of nucleating centres.

V. Miscellaneous Causes and Conditions

1. Hypothermia (Cooling of body to too low a temperature)
Cause: Though hypothermia is not confined to divers, being found in all situations where the human body is markedly cooled, it is a very serious risk in diving operations. If the core body (deep body) temperature drops below 35°-36° the diver is entering a region of risk which increases as the temperature of the deep body drops. Below core temperature of from 34°-35°C the risk becomes very serious. Below 33°-34°C death is usually imminent.
Subjective symptoms: (in order of increasing severity) Sensation of cold, sporadic shivering which can be suppressed by exercise of will-power, uncontrollable shivering, no shivering, amnesia, hallucinations, delusions, hardly conscious.
Objective symptoms: (in order of increasing severity) Pallor of skin as capillaries constrict, oxygen consumption rises, visible shivering at first occasional then continuous, cessation of shivering. Subject may lose consciousness, cardiac abnormalities, death. Note that once shivering has reached the uncontrollable stage, the victim is breathing very rapidly and may not have good enough co-ordination or strength to properly control his or her diving. Any diver seen in this state should be brought ashore or aboard with full assistance immediately, noting only that risk of decompression accident is a reason for not doing so.
Treatment: The basis is initially to prevent

further cooling and as soon as possible to apply external rewarming. Note that undressing the diver may place him in a situation of greater risk from wind cooling and that a diver in an open boat may be wind cooled, even when dressed in a wet suit, more rapidly than if he had remained in the water. So if in an open boat, cover diver with say anorak trousers and top or oilskins. When an appreciable source of heat for warming the victim is available, either bath him starting at 37°C and warming to 40°C ideally immersing trunk of body only, or if hot air above 40°C is available, undress victim, dry him if necessary, and expose to warm air. If conditions in any way doubtful, or if diver does not make a quick recovery, call medical help. In cases of slight hypothermia, hot drinks and a site out of the wind may be all that is needed.

2. Poisonous Animals
Note that with the exception of the Weaver fish, *Trachinus,* a bottom living fish, no really venomous animal is found in UK waters, but if stung by this or badly stung by jellyfish, consult medical advice. In other areas, consult local experts, before diving, about risks. A few people may have bad allergic reaction to marine organisms not normally considered hazardous.

3. Attacks by Predatory Animals
Very unlikely in UK waters though not unknown. Remove victim from water as soon as possible, apply first-aid consonant with degree of injury, calling medical help in serious cases.

VI. Drowning (Hypoxia Combined with Changes in Blood Composition)

Cause: Inhaling water. There are three types of drowning following inhalation of water. (a) When water does not enter lungs due to glottal spasm – known as Blue Drowning. (b) Saltwater entering lungs, and (c) Freshwater entering lungs. Both (b) and (c) are somtimes known as White Drowning.
Objective symptoms – BLUE DROWNING: Very like acute hypoxia; breathing may restart spontaneously.
Objective symptoms – WHITE DROWNING: Lips, ear lobes, nail beds and other parts of the skin very white. Breathing will have stopped. Some from amongst many other symptoms will be seen but it is hard to predict which in any given case.

If white drowning occurs in seawater, the seawater in the lungs tends to remove water from the blood stream, but this effect is not rapidly very serious. With freshwater in the lungs, the blood may take up water, this may lead to break-up of the blood cells and serious damage to the heart muscle, etc. Consequently with white drowning in freshwater, the victim may die more rapidly than does a case of white drowning in seawater. Blue drowning in either type of water, though serious, offers a better chance of successful resuscitation. However, the resuscitator should not take these differences into account, because precise diagnosis is a matter for experts and because successful resuscitation of seemingly unlikely cases has been achieved. Recognition of the type of drowning is usually very difficult for the resuscitator.

Treatment: Clear obstructions in airway followed by EAR or Silvester-Brosch method

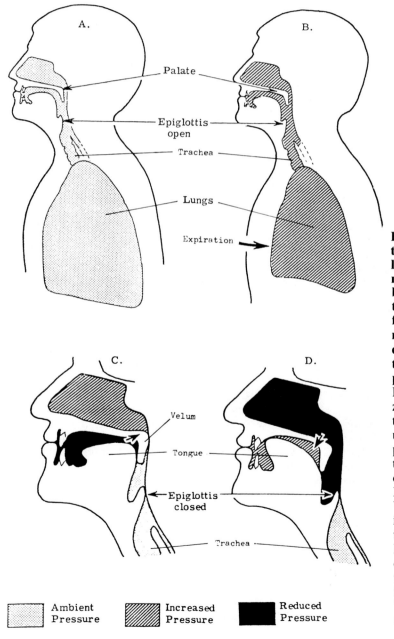

Figure 74. Ear clearing techniques. A. Air spaces in lungs, pharynx, mouth and nose of a diver in mid-breath. B. Earclearing by the Valsalva manoeuvre: by forcible expiration with the nose and mouth closed the diver raises the pressure in the air spaces above ambient pressure and thus opens the Eustachian tubes. C. Frenzel technique: by pushing the tongue backward and upwards the palate is pushed up which increases the pressure at the opening of the Eustachian tube (see Fig. 69 for position). D. Velar Depression: the palate is depressed by pushing the tongue forwards. This lowers the pressure near the opening of the Eustachian tube. Note that the epiglottis is closed in the Frenzel and Velar depression techniques.

if victim's face damaged. Heart (cardiac) massage if necessary and known by resuscitator. Continue EAR until victim recovers or medical practitioner tells you to stop. If victim does not recover and it is impossible to contact a medical practitioner, continue EAR for at least 2 hours. If the victim responds, he or she must be taken to a medical practitioner because of possible after effects.

C. EAR CLEARING TECHNIQUES

1. Valsalva Manoeuvre

This, perhaps the most widely known method, is now not recommended because there is some risk of fainting or even of producing pulmonary barotrauma. In this technique, the diver exhales forcibly against a closed nose and mouth. The raised air pressure in the Eustachian tube should open it to the middle ear. (It also causes the heart to partially empty and thus leads to fainting; air pressure in the lungs rises.)

2. Velar Depression. See Fig. 74

The velum i.e. soft palate at the top of the mouth can be depressed particularly if you press the tip of your tongue hard against the front top of the palate. The resulting decrease in pressure in nasal and pharyngeal regions and the accompanying jaw movement open the Eustachian tube. Rather difficult to learn, but very safe and effective. Nose or mouth sealing not required. Glottis must be voluntarily closed. In another version of this, velum is raised and the increase in air pressure opens the tubes.

3. Frenzel Manoeuvre. See Fig. 74

If the mass of the tongue can be pulled back, with the tip on the top of the mouth, the resulting increase in air pressure in the nasal and pharygeal passages and jaw movement opens the Eustachian tube. Difficult but safe. Glottis has to be voluntarily closed and mouth and nose may need to be closed. Contract muscles of floor of mouth and neck and pull tongue which should be at top of mouth backwards.

4. Voluntary Opening of Eustachian Tubes

This is the hardest method to learn but the most effective one of all. If you can move muscles at the back and sides of your throat and this produces a quivering feeling and sound in your ears, you have succeeded.

Chapter 5

Deep diving recommendations

The NDC recognises that there are basically three different types of deep dive.

1. Dives to depths between 30 and 45 m depth carried out with the intention of avoiding any need for decompression.

2. Dives to depths between 30 and 45 m depth carried out with the intention of spending time at depth so that decompression stops may or will be necessary.

3. Dives to depths beyond 45 m which will almost certainly require the need for decompression stops and where problems of nitrogen narcosis are likely to be present. If the dive is to be beyond 50 m prior approval from the N.D.C. is required.

The first type of dive though not undemanding requires less ability, equipment and organisation than the second or third types. Type 3 dives are the most demanding.

All types of dive require the basic expedition organisation laid down for all diving expeditions. Normal diving rules apply of course to all deep dives. Type 1 dives have requirements additional to the basic rules, Type 2 and 3 dives require extra rules in addition to the Type 1 rules. Type 3 dives have rules which assume the application of the rules for types 2 and 1. See below.

TYPE 1. 'BOUNCE', *i.e.* NO-DECOMPRESSION DIVES IN THE RANGE 30-45m

Equipment

Aqualung of capacity such that the diver will have 25 cubic feet of air left in the set at the start of the ascent. We have noted that a surprisingly large number of people are trying to dive in the 30-45 m range with sets of capacity as low as 50 to 60 cubic feet of air. Unless your air consumption is phenomenally low, sets of such small capacity simply do not give enough time at depth for one diver to search for or/and rescue a fellow diver. A rough and ready rule might be that sets should be of a minimum of 70 cubic feet capacity for such dives. It is highly

desirable that the air comes from compressors that are regularly tested for carbon dioxide and carbon monoxide contamination. An ABLJ or stab jacket with a fully charged cylinder and/or direct feed must be worn. Regulator neck straps must be removed so that sharing can be carried out without delay. Octopus (i.e. 2 mouthpiece) regulators, or even better separate complete regulators on each of two cylinders give added safety but neither of these procedures totally remove the need to share. A depth gauge, a torch and a watch must be carried. Flashing lights could be used by the diver for added safety as would an electronic dive timer/maximum depth recorder.

Training

Minimum qualification. 3rd class diver who has completed the 2nd class tests on shared ascents and rescue, and who has demonstrated her or his ability to use an ABLJ (including breathing from it at depths of 15 m at least) to their BDO previously or to use a stab jacket in the same way.

Experience

Each diver must have had appreciable experience of dives to depths within 12 m of the proposed depth of the deep dive. 'Appreciable' means not less than two dives within the previous fortnight and four within the previous two months to within 12 m of the target depth for the dive. The reason for this recommendation lies in the fact that many diving accidents have had as their main cause lack of fitness or familiarity with the water. It's asking for trouble to leave off diving for three months and then rush off to do a 36 m dive.

The requirements for familiarity with an ABLJ is based on the fact that an ABLJ provides a final line of safety in the event of an accident beause it provides an independent breathing supply and considerable buoyancy. In addition we consider that an ABLJ should be used to maintain a wet-suited diver at close to to neutral buoyancy during a normal deep dive. A marked degree of negative buoyancy at depth has been a cause of a number of diving accidents. If a dry-suited diver loses buoyancy through faulty seals or tears from his suit the ABLJ or stab jacket provides an emergency source of buoyancy. The dry suit diver should try to keep his weight belt loading low, certainly below the lift capacity of the ABLJ or stab jacket.

Dive Planning

The planning of deep dives is rather more complex than quite a number of divers have supposed. This very complexity, however, makes the planning something of a challenge, and the successful completion of a dive should give a sense of achievement to the expedition leader. The first two points to be borne in mind are (a) that normal diving rules apply to deep dives as well as to others and (b) that all deep dives may require decompression procedures unless very definite rules are made and followed for each individual dive. The Expedition leader must have ascertained the maximum and general depths at the dive site at the time of the dive so that no-decompression limits can be established. Use of sounding gear or consultation of a chart and tide tables will probably be essential to do this. Even if the site is well known to the Expedition leader he or she should bear in mind the effect of the tide on the actual depth that is going to be found. Once the maximum duration of no-decompression dives has been worked out the Expedition leader must then decide on dive durations which will (a) be considerably shorter than the no-decompression limits so that there will be no need to run into decompression time even if the dive is prolonged by say five to ten minutes and (b) suit the size of aqualung sets being used by the divers.

The Expedition leader must take more than usual care to check that the divers who propose to dive deep do have the equipment and qualifications required. He must inform them of the proposed dive duration, the no-decompression limit and the duration and depths of the stops required should they slightly exceed the limits.

Weather and water conditions affect deep dives to a greater extent than shallower dives. Currents, in particular descending currents, are a particular hazard to the deep diver and normally care should be taken to ensure that deep dives are made at slack water. If a deep dive has to be made in a current, shot lines and distance lines are essential. If the dive is made close to shore with the divers following the side of an underwater cliff it may be possible to make this sort of deep dive without the use of a shot line, provided of course there are no appreciable currents. If however, the dive is made some way off shore or if there is no clear under water feature to provide directional clues underwater, a shot line with a distance line should be used. Stop marks and, if necessary spare sets, can be fixed on the shot line at the correct depths. It should be remembered that diving accidents have happened either because the shot line had so little buoyancy at the top that the divers dragged the float underwater as they tried to climb up it, or because there was so little weight at the bottom, the line either dragged away or the divers could not make a stop because the line floated up. 30 kg on the bottom and 20 kg buoyancy on the surface are about right.

The deep divers should be in pairs and they and their cover should not be mingled together with other divers in the water. Further deep dives should not be carried out in exactly the same sight as the first unless it is known that the site is free from sediment. Particular care must be taken to record times of the start and finish of the dive. A prearranged dive duration should have been agreed between beachmaster, expedition leader and divers which avoids the need to decompress. If the divers do not return to the surface within 5 minutes of this time the standby diver (preferably with a companion) should start a search. The standby diver must meet the qualifications required for deep dives. Decompression tables and spare aqualung sets must be available on site. Repeat dives are not to be undertaken without the agreement of the Expedition leader and advice to the beachmaster and precise application of the decompression procedure must be clearly understood.

There are considerable advantages in putting divers down a cliff when practice deep dives are being made. It provides a clear set of reference points which can be returned to even on a low grade bearing. It usually provides many points at which decompression stages can be carried out. It is much harder to find a shot in the open water once it's out of sight and once you've lost it decompression stops become harder, though, of course, you should be on the distance line in such a situation.

Dive Conduct

Though a dive leader should be appointed the two divers should act much more as equals in this type of dive than in any other.

The dive shall be abandoned if:

1. If appreciable currents exist or if the dive site is much deeper than expected and there are any difficulties in holding the desired depth.

2. If either diver knows that he or she is becoming narcosed or sees signs of this in another diver. Any diver feeling apprehension should give the ascent signal and terminate the dive.

3. If the depth gauges or decompression meters (if used) differ appreciably in their readings.

During the descent brief stops should be made to (a) exchange OK signals and (b) to restore buoyancy. Probably two such stops will be necessary before 30m depth is reached and rather more for purpose (a) down from 30-45m. Probably only one buoyancy adjustment will need to be made between 30m and 45m. Ascent should be started before no-decompression limits are exceeded and while 25'[3] remains in the sets (whichever happens first). During ascent air should be bled off from ABLJs or dry suits particularly at about 12m. Divers should be slightly overweight at 3m depth with nearly all the air used and deflated ABLJs and/or nearly deflated dry suits so that open water decompression can be carried out if necessary. Divers should not be more than 3 kg negative on the bottom with the ABLJ or/and dry suit deflated and weight belt off: a rather harder matter to establish. The reason for this is to ensure that emergency ascents can easily be done after dropping weight belts if ABLJ or suit buoyancy control does not function.

Each diver will know and have agreed the no-decompression limit and the duration and depths of stops if the limit is slightly exceeded. Many watches have bezels that slip during a dive and thus it may be a good idea to record times of entry and start of ascent on a diver's slate or use a dive timer. One's memory at 45m is not too reliable.

One of the main problems with deep diving happens if divers lose each other at depth. When this happens you may not know whether your companion has rushed off to the surface, whether he is happily swimming around just too far away to be seen, oblivious of your absence, or whether he has sunk further in distress. Since the surface is so far off free ascents are pretty difficult and are really last resorts in emergency. On losing contact each diver should switch on his light or flasher and rotate light and himself twice around, slowly, looking upwards and downwards. If he sees the other diver's light, fin towards it. If contact is not made the next action should be to search downwards for 6m if this can be done, and around the site for 2 minutes over a radius of about 6m. If contact is still not made slowly ascend. If you are unable to hear the other diver, do not assume he has surfaced: his demand valve might have stopped working. There are several reasons for this recommendation which differs from the normal (shallow water) practice on losing your companion. The main reason is because it is going to take a long time to ascend to the surface and longer still if you have to descend again because your companion has not been able to get up. If the other diver has not surfaced when you surface alert the standby divers immediately. Because of the problems that arise once contact is lost, divers should take particular care to keep close together during deep dives. Surface cover of deep dives will often find it difficult to see bubbles ascending from the divers, because the bubbles tend to be very small on reaching the surface from depth. If they lose sight of the bubbles they should notify the dive marshal, who should (a) start a search for the bubbles and (b) inform the Expedition leader who will decide whether to start a rescue search with his standby divers. He will in any event start a rescue if the divers have not surfaced by a prearranged time.

Use of a buddy-line might be considered as means of keeping divers together on a deep dive. However, it should be borne in mind that use of a buddy-line requires some practice. Buddy-lines if used should be fastened by quick release clips to the harness of each diver. Hand held buddy-lines will probably be dropped in emergency or when a diver is narcosed.

TYPE 2. DIVES REQUIRING DECOMPRESSION PROCEDURES

This type of dive of course includes those dives in which there is uncertainty as to whether decompression procedures will or will not be needed. Normal diving rules and requirements for Type 1 dives are of course to be followed unless there is conflict with the recommendations set out below. This type of dive should be avoided wherever possible.

Personal Equipment

Aqualungs of capacity at least 80 cubic feet should be used. Sets or demand valves must have contents gauges. As in Type 1 dives an ABLJ or constant volume suit, depth gauges, torches and watches must be carried. Neck straps must be removed from single hose valves. Decompression meters, slates and flashing lights could in addition be used.

Training

The minimum qualification is 2nd class diver plus proven ability to breathe from an ABLJ or stab jacket at 12m. The divers should have recently made Type 1 dives to the depth of the planned dive. If dry suits are used, divers must be experienced in their use.

Dive planning and special equipment

The prime requirements for dive safety when decompression procedures are to be used are (a) a sufficient supply of air (or other breathing mixture) to ensure that the whole decompression schedule can be carried out (b) a system that ensures that the divers will return to the position and depth at which decompression is to be carried out with certainty and (c) a method of ensuring that the decompression stops are carried out for the correct times at the correct depth. These requirements mean that a lot of pre-dive planning has to be done to ensure that all the correct equipment and information is available on site. All dives of this type should be planned as dives to a known depth for a set time, sufficient to do the job in hand without incurring exceptionally long decompression procedures. It should be remembered that long decompressions are at least boring and chilling (in Scottish waters) and can be hazardous if for example the weather deteriorates during the process.

Air supply

The size of the sets used by each diver should be sufficient to meet the requirements of the planned dive, and hence planned decompression with a margin to allow for the demands of undue physical exertion, small errors in timing and depth and accident. A 20 per cent margin would probably be desirable. Sets must be fixed on a shot line at the depth either of the only or first stop expected to be used. (When more than one stop is used time on the first

stop is usually very short so that it is unlikely that the diver will need to switch to it during that stop.) There should be one for each diver in the deep dive. Sets should be easily detachable from the line so that they can be carried up to shallower or if necessary down to deeper stops or put on; quick release clips (carabineer clips) might be used. Sets used should allow at least one hour's decompression time. Remember that a 24 minute dive to 42m will require 30 minutes decompression with the first stop at 10m.

Ensuring the return of the divers to the correct decompression depth and position

This is usually best done with a shot line though other methods such as lines rigged on a rock face (as in cave-diving) or ultrasonic beacons may be essential or preferable in special cases. If necessary a distance line can be run from the shot bottom to the work position. Divers descend the shot and work out to the dive position with a distance line and return to decompression position which is on the shot line. Rigging the shot line requires a boat, even if deep water is very close to shore. It is very important to ensure that the shot has sufficient buoyancy at the surface to prevent overweight divers and sets dragging it underwater, and sufficient bottom weight to prevent underweight divers dragging it up or wind or current dragging it off position. The length of shot should allow for changes in tide height during the dive but not be so long that it runs at a shallow angle. Bottom weight should be at least 40 kg and surface buoyancy at least 20 kg. Several fatal accidents have occurred in other diving clubs owing to shot lines being given insufficient surface buoyancy or bottom weight. Only one dive at a time (of 2 to 3 divers) should be on the shot.

Correct application of decompression tables

It is essential that the divers follow the correct decompression schedule. Obviously it is much easier to do this if the divers are in some form of communication with the surface. The Dive Marshal can then time the dive and inform the divers of the stops and their duration (and vice-versa). In general terms the Dive Marshal will have agreed the approximate length of the dive with the divers and informed them of the decompression schedule for this dive before they start the dive. In practice there are only two methods of surface communication open to amateurs. The first is rope signals, which are slow and difficult to use with long messages. The alternative is to lower a message on a slate or to send it down with a standby diver. The divers might find it a help to carry details of their planned decompression on a slate with them. Both they and the dive marshals time the dive. This requires that either the divers signal the surface on reaching the first decompression stop or that a standby diver observes their arrival, checks that they are OK and then surfaces to inform the dive marshal. The dive marshal should inform the divers of the length of their dive and the decompression (revised if their dive is longer or shorter than planned). If possible a standby diver enters the water shortly before the planned end of the dive and awaits and times the arrival of the divers at the first stop. If they fail to arrive on time he signals the surface. If they are more than five minutes late rescue (emergency) procedure is followed. This standby should remain at or below the first stop while others are carrying out the rescue. Once divers ascend to this position he signals the surface. If, however, the divers return towards the surface at or just before the planned time the Dive Marshal sends down a signal that the agreed procedure is to be followed. If the dive returns early the Dive Marshal sends down a revised schedule as soon as possible. If there is any disagreement about the duration of dive between marshal and divers the longer duration should be the one followed in decompression. All this also requires that the Dive Marshal carries a copy of the decompression tables with him, and is thoroughly conversant with their use. The Dive Marshal should not do any work with the boat while he is supervising the dive, all his attention should be given to the dive. He will have previously ascertained the whereabouts of the nearest telephone, doctor and decompression chamber.

Emergency procedures

The emergency procedures (dive conduct) shall be based on that set out for Type 1 dives. Greater care should be taken to make towards the surface at or before the agreed duration of the dive. If the dive runs over time appreciably it may be necessary to make the first stop at a deeper point than originally planned (this may lead to all manner of difficulties). In addition the amount of air required for decompression will be considerably increased.

TYPE 3 DIVES, I.E. THOSE BEYOND 45M

All that has been said for type 2 dives applies here. A shot must be used even if the dive is to be no more than a 'bounce' (Dives over 45m will almost certainly need decompression stages). Training, fitness and planning need to be of a high standard for such dives and divers planning to make such dives should work up towards them through type 1 and 2 dives.

Sets of 2.5m³ (100 cubic foot) capacity should be used. Divers should have demonstrated their ability to carry out deep rescue to their BDO before type 3 dives (see note of deep rescue). Even if timings and DCP meters indicate no need for a stop a precautionary stop of 5 minutes at 3m should be carried out. Repeat dives are most inadvisable for 12 hours after a type 3 dive and if essential (for rescue) great care should be taken with subsequent decompression.

Standby divers for type 2 and 3 dives should be experienced in these types of dives because they may be needed for rescue (see discussion of type 1 dives). A less experienced diver can be used to service the divers during their decompression stages as long as a fully experienced one is also available for rescue work. If the dive is to be to depths greater than 50m prior approval from the NDC is required.

Electronic decompression meters

Though the utility of such instruments seems obvious especially for deep dives, the high incidence of bends incidents with such meters, has at the time of writing, led the SSAC to recommend that these meters be used as depth and time recorders.

Chapter 6

Expedition Organisation.

INTRODUCTION

The reasons for running diving expeditions are to provide dives which are safer, more interesting, more suited to a variety of ability and experience and which provide a larger element of further learning than would be obtained if you dived singly or in pairs. We have already given a short and elementary description of expedition organisation in Chapter 3, but now we return to the subject and treat it in some detail.

Diving expeditions must of course avoid accident but an expedition is a success only if everyone concerned returns saying that they enjoyed the day and dive and that they individually learnt something about diving from it. Running diving expeditions is, of course, the overall responsibility of the Branch Diving Officer, but unless he has a fantastic amount of free time and perfect health, he or she will need to delegate organisation to other members of the Branch from time to time. Furthermore, an expedition, if properly run, is very much safer than other forms of diving, diving alone being, of course, highly foolish.

THE BASIC ORGANISATION OF AN EXPEDITION

The essential feature in setting up an expedition is to ensure that there is a chain of responsibility. Divers normally dive in pairs or occasionally in triplets, the Dive Leader being in charge. Each diver operates to increase his or her own and the other's safety and enjoyment. They do this in such simple matters as staying together underwater so that they don't waste time looking for each other or hazard themselves by being alone and out of sight of another diver. If possible the Dive Leader will be someone who knows the site and can lead those who don't. Divers also dive together so that if one has an accident or mishap, the other can help. The chain of responsibility is continued with the person carrying out snorkel or boat cover. Both the cover and the divers report to the Dive Marshal (Beachmaster) at the start and end of each dive that all is well. If it is not, the Dive Marshal either receives a report from those concerned and informs the Expedition Leader and if necessary the Safety Officer and the standby diver(s). If no report is made by a prearranged time, the Dive Marshal arranges a search. The chain of responsibility is shown in diagram in Fig. 75. Responsibility runs in both directions. The Expedition Leader is responsible for safety and enjoyment. So he is responsible to you for your safety and enjoyment. You are responsible to him in making sure that events happen and reports are made when they should.

LIMITATIONS ON DIVES

All who plan to run expeditions should remember that various constraints limit their expeditions. Chief amongst these constraints are:

1. The number and qualifications of the divers who are likely to attend. Obviously if the Expedition Leader is the only non-trainee diver, he or she is going to have a very hard time to run more than two dives (of say at most four other people) of fairly short duration. If this situation is likely to arise, invite your Regional Coach and ask him to bring along a few other qualified divers or join up with another Branch for the outing. Again, if the dive is an arduous one demanding deep diving experience (see Chapter 8), it is useless bringing along more than a small number of 3rd Class divers because they will just be unable to take part in the deep diving and so prevent the deep diving or hang around doing nothing much. (A few of them might be used in tending divers at decompression stops.)

2. The number and qualifications of the divers who actually turn up.

3. Problems caused by the nature of the dive site. Often these will present little problem, but if the site can only be reached by a

fifty minute inflatable trip, you will get few divers on to it unless you can provide several inflatables. Again the site may constrain diving to a short period because of currents, or on a particular day it may be so exposed to the weather that diving is impossible or becomes impossible during the dive.

4. Changes in the weather. Though it is unusual, it is not unknown for the wind to rise *from 0 to force 7 in 15 minutes* and if this happens during a dive, those who surface into suddenly rough seas may be surprised. In general terms, the Expedition Leader should, from forecasts and a watch on the weather at the site decide (*a*) whether any diving is going to be attempted, and (*b*) whether the wind or at least its effect on the site is increasing or decreasing.

Reading these four paragraphs should immediately indicate to you that dive planning must be flexible. For example, you should have planned an alternative site to use nearby if the weather deteriorates or if too many inexperienced and too few experienced divers come.

TYPES OF EXPEDITION

Differing types of expedition make differing claims on the need for planning, on the manpower required and on the equipment needed at site. When planning an expedition you must match your intentions to the numbers and to the skill of the divers available as well as to such matters as the equipment needed. Above all, you must have the agreement of your divers that the sort of expedition you envisage is one they wish to have as well. Thus BDOs should always discuss their proposed dives with members of the Branch, particularly perhaps with active members of the Branch Committee, well before they happen. These discussions need, of course, to be nothing more than outline discussions. Sometimes it may be desirable to call a meeting at which all interested members of the Branch can put their views.

On many occasions, an expedition will be simply no more than a day's outing for about a dozen people of variable experience and diving ability. Probably some of the divers will be trainees or of very little experience. On such expeditions, it is common to devote a good deal of effort to training and testing. Others may dive on the simple basis of looking to see what's there. If these expeditions can

have an element of diving with a specific objective, such as food collection, underwater photography, wreck or site surveying, they become more interesting.

If the dive has a specific purpose such as minor salvage, searching for lost objects, collecting specimens for marine biologists, etc., the Expedition Leader will have to ensure that his dive plans include ways of, and perhaps equipment for, tackling the task.

On other occasions, or indeed on some occasions including the tasks mentioned above, the diving planned may require abilities found only in experienced divers of 3rd, or when it is more difficult still, of 2nd or even 1st Class standard. Expedition Leaders should bear in mind that each of the features mentioned in the following list makes diving more difficult and thus extra experience necessary:

1. Deep water, especially over 30m depth.
2. Currents or risk of currents during dive, in excess of ½ knot.
3. Diving in caves, or inside wrecks.
4. Diving in very low visibility.
5. Diving amongst ropes, lines, etc.
6. Roped divers using rope signals.
7. Various types of work underwater.
8. Strong seas.
9. Boat activity on the surface.

In some cases the level of experience required has been precisely laid down by the SSAC, for instance with deep dives, see Chapter 8. In other cases no precise ruling has been made but the EL should either have appropriate experience or discuss the matter beforehand with those more experienced than he or she. Obviously if several of these factors are present simultaneously, at one dive site, they add together to make the dive still more difficult.

On occasion, the desire to carry out a relatively advanced type of dive will lead to some problems in handling inexperienced divers. It may be necessary to exclude them from a dive, but this should only be done when you are fairly sure that there is no way that they can enjoy some relatively easy and safe diving at the same time. If a Branch runs a number of advanced dives, its trainees may feel neglected, so their needs should not be forgotten and suitable dives run for them possibly with another Branch.

Finally there are those expeditions that last longer than a day, often abroad or to remote sites. These require, of course, very much more planning than the average one day expedition dealt with in this chapter, but the same basic principles apply to the diving in long term expeditions as in one day ones; the differences in planning refer, of course, mainly to transport, feeding and accommodation and to the servicing and repair of equipment and compressed air provision.

PREREQUISITES FOR AN EXPEDITION

These are quite simple:

1. A group of divers of adequate training and experience. This requirement does not imply that all the divers must necessarily be experienced, though some dive sites will require this, see below, but that there should be enough experienced divers to allow the inexperienced to dive with enjoyment and safety.

2. Appropriate equipment available, both in terms of diving equipment for individual divers and if a boat or boats is used the basic equipment which goes with a boat, see Chapter 10.

3. A suitable dive site. Dive sites can be classed according to the sort of experience and ability required to dive safely in normal weather conditions. This has been done for sites quoted in the 'Guide to Scottish Dive Sites' published serially in *Scottish Diver*, starting in 1979. The grading is quoted there.

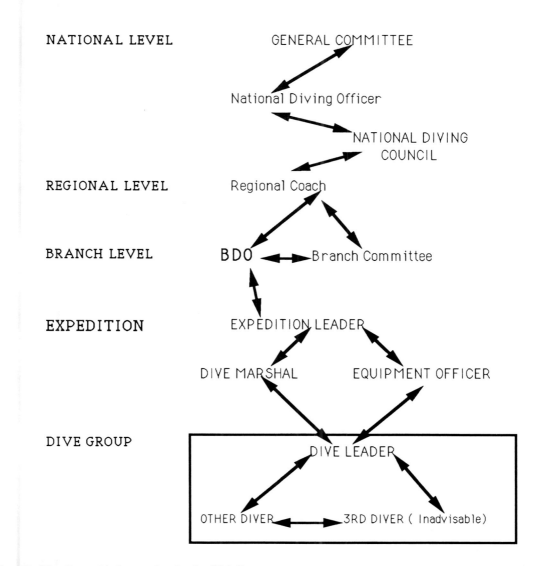

Fig. 75. The flow of information in the SSAC.

Most BDOs will know approximately how many divers and their various degrees of experience he or she is likely to have on an expedition in the next few months. The BDO will also probably know a number of sites or have suggested a number of sites your Branch has not visited yet. In most cases, he or she will have some idea of their suitability for the divers who are likely to attend. These facts can be used to announce a dive programme for several months ahead. In some cases it may be noted that certain sites will require very good weather conditions for a dive, while other sites may be immune from hazards from all but the very worst weather.

INITIAL PLANNING OF AN EXPEDITION

In the period of two to four days immediately prior to an expedition, the Expedition Leader, who will either be the BDO or another member appointed by the BDO, needs to make sure that he or she knows various facts about the proposed dive and to make preliminary plans.

The site itself

How far from shore does it lie? Is a boat essential or desirable for transport? Is the site subject to currents? What weather conditions might prevent a dive? What is the average depth of the water? Are there any problems about access to the site?

The personnel

Who has said that they will come and what is their diving experience? Is it easy to make up lists of dive leaders and their companions or is there a shortage of experienced personnel such that there may be difficulties in organising a dive? The EL may well take decisions about who will fill which of the officer's duties on the dive.

Equipment

The EL should make a list of the equipment he or she thinks will be necessary and checks with the Equipment Officer. A Check list is given in this chapter, see Fig. 76.

All these questions and matters need attention by the EL using the sources set out below.

Fig. 76. Check-list for Equipment Officers for equipment needed for a dive expedition

1. Safety Equipment always required:

Aqualung cylinder(s) and regulators for use in case of decompression problem or if an extended search for a missing person is needed.

1st Aid Kit.

Dive Flag (with line and pole to fly it clearly).

Dive log-sheet (and protective cover).

Watch to time dives.

2. Safety Equipment which may be required:

Torches.

Surface marker buoys and lines to be towed by divers.

Light line for rigging underwater or for 'buddy lines'.

Safety equipment for small boats (see Ch. 10 for detailed list).

Shot lines, weights and surface buoys.

3. Equipment for convenience of members:

Such aqualung cylinders, demand valves and weight belts as they may require.

Lifejackets, surface or ABLJ.

Equipment required for tests, e.g. search lines.

Boat(s), outboards and other ancillary equipment.

Spare 'O' rings, silicone grease and small tools for general light repairs.

Finding out about the dive site

The following sources should be of value:
1. Talking to those who know the site.
2. Using the OS 1:50,000 map to judge road access to the site and to get some idea that you have chosen a beach or easy entry to put your boat or divers in and out of the water. You can also use this map to get an idea about the exposure of the site to the wind, for example if your site is in the lee of a fairly high island, say 100m high or so, there will probably be a good wind shadow on the NE side of the island in a strong SW breeze.
3. Using a chart of the area. Charts at the scales of 1:25,000 to 1:75,000 give a great deal of detail which is useful for the diver. Charts at greater scales do not contain enough fine detail to be of much use. Unfortunately not all areas are covered at the 1:25,000 or even the 1:75,000 scale. If you do not understand the symbols on the chart obtain the chart or booklets which explain them. A few areas are detailed in 1:10,000 or even 1:5000 scales; such charts are very useful to divers but tend to be confined to details of port areas. One of the most important pieces of information you can extract from a chart is the probable depth of water at the site. Remember that chart depths are given as soundings or contours below chart datum. Chart datum is detailed on each particular chart and is usually close to water level at an extremely low water spring tide. Obviously you must remember to add the tidal depth at any particular time of the tide to the chart datum to get the real depth in which you plan to dive. Details of the method of doing this are given in Chapter 7 as well as in many books on navigation. Underwater contours, though only approximate, may for example, indicate attractive underwater cliffs or flat half-dismal mud bottoms. In addition the chart will usually give you some idea of the nature of the bottom of the site, i.e. sand, mud, stone, rock, etc. Wrecks are often marked, but usually rather inaccurately so that divers may have trouble in finding them; in addition, of course, there is no guarantee from a 'Wk' symbol that anything much will now be there. Decay, salvage, or further break up by the sea may have removed nearly all of a wreck. If the letters (P.A.) follow the 'Wk' symbol, the meaning is 'position approximate' and this should make you appreciate that it is still less likely that you will find a wreck from that symbol.

Charts are also valuable in the information they give you about tidal currents. Often these are marked by arrows, those with fletching mark ebb currents, with a printed estimate of the speed beside them, Fuller information may be given for one or more tidal diamonds marked on the chart in the form of tables at the side or bottom of the chart. These tables give hour by hour estimates of current direction and speed for both spring (maximum) and neap (minimum) conditions. Note however that currents change a lot both in intensity and in timing close inshore and information at a diamond may be inapplicable a few km. away 20m from shore. Further useful information on currents can be obtained from the various Admiralty Pilot Books.

Personnel

If you are running a Branch or Club dive it will help if you can get intending divers to sign themselves up for the dive some days earlier. Obviously your group will have to have developed a regular system for doing this. A regular notice posted at each pool session stating where, when and who is running the next dive and inviting signatures and details of equipment requirements etc., will help you a lot. You can ask those who sign to contact you by phone the day before the actual dive so that you can be pretty sure of final numbers. If you just rely on people turning up on the day at a meeting place you may get into difficulties, if for example you need an exact number of divers, say for a hired boat or if you need a certain number of BTPs for some training project. In such cases you will need to organise your dives with greater care and forethought than you have previously.

Officers for the dive

This title sounds very official but you will need to appoint various people to carry out assigned duties to help you run the dive safely. The Equipment Officer should be appointed at an early date for he or she will be responsible for bringing all Branch equipment needed for the dive. She or he will also be responsible for bringing it back. The Equipment Officer will need to know at this stage whether a boat dive is planned, how many Branch aqualungs, regulators, ABLJs and weight belts will be needed on site, etc. He or she will need to liaise with the Branch Equipment Officer(s) and with the individual members who are going to need the equipment. So it will probably be a good idea if they write in their individual requirements on the expedition booking list. Once the Equipment Officer has the list, he or she can make definite plans.

Meanwhile the Expedition Leader should start making more definite plans about the other officers he needs, though these need not, indeed normally probably should not, be announced until everybody has met together at the dive or launching site. Preplanning at this stage is a good idea since it avoids delay and allows calm appreciation of many problems that might arise. Work out your plans early but do not be rigid in them, change them to suit events should events change from expectation when you are on site. Trying to devise the best way to run an expedition when everyone is impatient to start diving is a recipe for a poor dive, indeed perhaps a dangerous dive.

The Expedition Leader will need to appoint a Deputy Leader who will act while he or she is actually diving. A Deputy may only be needed for a short time but should be a person of experience and competence because an emergency might arise while the Leader is diving, even though this is unlikely.

Dive Marshal

One or more Dive Marshals (Beachmasters) are appointed to ensure that an accurate log is kept of all dives. There are three main and one auxiliary reason for keeping this record.

1. A Dive log provides a way of checking immediately the whereabouts of each diver. Thus the log is used to check the progress of the dive and ensure that the right persons are ready at the same time to start each dive. But the greatest importance of the log is that it allows a check to discover if any diver is missing or overdue. If the Dive Marshal detects or suspects this, he tells the Expedition Leader or his Deputy immediately. They then begin to organise measures to meet these potential or real hazards.

2. The Dive Marshal uses the record to check that none of the divers could be at risk from decompression sickness. Thus all divers report to the Dive Marshal after returning from a dive. They tell him their maximum depth and time. He confirms the duration of the dive beause he or his assistants have timed the moment at which they signalled descent (OK signal to shore or boat) and re-signalled the end of the dive (ditto). The Dive Marshal then uses depth and time data to check that no one has exceeded the no-stop limits (or in the event of a dive with decompression stops that these have been correctly followed). If any definite or possible discrepancy is found and there appears to be a need for decompression the Dive Marshal informs the divers and helps them to carry this out as soon as possible. He also informs the Expedition Leader of the problem and so long as the divers have no symptoms of decompression sickness they return to the water aided by stand-by divers and by the provision of spare sets (if necessary).

3. In the unlikely event of a serious or fatal accident, the records kept by the Dive Marshal would form an essential piece of evidence.

4. The records kept by the Dive Marshal are given at the end of the dives to the Expedition Leader who uses them in preparation of the dive report. In turn they may be forwarded to the Branch Training Officer or BDO for use in keeping training records.

The Dive Marshal need not be a person who is diving; indeed if they are of a careful and methodical nature and can understand a decompression table, they need not be a diver at all. But remember that the Dive Marshal must be out and about at all times. If the weather is bad, he or she may well get cold, wet or bored. If this happens, your Dive Marshal may be less than fully competent and certainly a bit resentful, so Expedition Leaders may need to have a standby Dive Marshal. It is a good idea to have the Dive Marshal check that divers are properly kitted, see Check list Fig. 77. But Dive Leaders always do this as well and the Equipment Officer may act instead of the Dive Marshal.

Dive Leader(s)

Dive Leaders are responsible for the safety of the divers in their group while in the water. Of course each person in a dive group is mutually responsible for the safety of the others, but there must be a single person who is responsible for deciding what is done at each stage of the dive. This person is the Dive Leader. His or her actions for safe diving are paramount, but DLs should also ensure that their group has an interesting dive, achieving their objects and that, if needed, any member of the dive is examined for any diving test that is, appropriately, required.

Normally, of course, the Dive Leader should be of greater experience than those he leads but it should be appreciated that there are many exceptions to this rule: e.g. divers taking the Dive Leader test, or divers with special local knowledge should lead those who do not know the site if any difficulties are anticipated etc. Normally those of middling experience should dive together. Obviously the more experienced will not wish to spend all their time diving with trainees so do let them on occasion have the more interesting dives that experienced divers can have if they dive together unhampered by trainees. If tests for the first set of qualifying dives for 3rd Class are being carried out by a trainee the Dive Leader will be a BTP of Grade 1 (Branch) or Grade 2 (Club) Instructor.

How do we recognise experience? Obviously possession of the qualifications of a 2nd Class diver (or a higher qualification) indicates that the diver has considerable knowledge. Experience is knowledge plus recent practical use of a wide range of techniques plus an ability to assess and react quickly to a diving problem plus the fitness to work well and, if need be hard, in the water. Thus as might be expected research has shown that it is the diver who has dived a lot recently who is the experienced diver. Note however that you may be an experienced diver in say Scottish waters but if you suddenly moved to say Jamaican waters you would be initially inexperienced as techniques there are necessarily not exactly the same as those in Scotland. Above all, bear in mind that a diver with less than 25 dives in total in a variety of conditions, or with less than six dives in the past three months cannot be described as experienced. These people should not lead dives unless their companion is more experienced. If their dive total is less than ten dives, they must not lead dives. The duties of Dive Leaders are as follows:

(i) they should check that their divers are properly kitted (see check list, Fig. 77), and should get one of their divers to check their own kitting-up.

(ii) they should explain the purpose and proposed progress of the dive, remarking in particular on any special features such as depth or time limitation or known hazards.

(iii) then they lead their party into the water or onto the boat to the dive site.

(iv) when ready to descend, the leader checks that everyone is ready and signals to Dive Marshal on shore or boat that they are about to dive.

(v) underwater the Dive Leader checks that everyone is present and signals OK and then leads the group in the planned direction, once the members of his party have returned the OK signal.

(vi) periodically the Dive Leader checks contents gauges and that the other divers are OK. The frequency of checking depends upon the experience of the other divers and on the depth.

(vii) as the preplanned dive duration expires or air contents fall to 30 BAR, whichever happens first, the Dive Leader starts surfacing procedure. On surfacing, the Dive Leader signals OK (or otherwise if appropriate) to the Dive Marshal.

(viii) ashore or on the boat the Dive Leader reports briefly on the dive to the Dive Marshal giving details of maximum depth, duration, etc. They also check that everyone in the group keeps together and that the aims of the dive are being achieved.

The Safety Officer

The prime duties of this officer are to handle the shore or boat based side should an accident occur. Thus he or she is primarily responsible for contacting doctor, police, coastguard or recompression chamber and must have obtained the appropriate telephone numbers and whereabouts of phones, etc. before diving starts. He or she will also handle first aid and may handle the checking of kitting up by divers (though this may well be left to the Dive Marshal). The Safety Officer's duties will usually be light, but should an accident occur, he or she must be immediately available for hard work, and must know what to do. The Safety Officer does not have to be a trained diver.

Boat-handlers

These persons need not be divers, but must be familiar with handling small boats amongst divers, with diving signals and with diving procedures. Boat handlers may easily get cold or bored so that a wise Expedition Leader plans their use to avoid this.

Stand-by Divers

A fully-kitted diver ready to go into the water should be available on boat or shore during each dive. The purpose of this diver is to effect rescue should an accident occur or be suspected. Obviously the stand-by diver should, if possible, be a diver who has not dived. The reason for this is that they should be warm and without any penalty for possible need for decompression. If they have dived, they may be less effective for both these reasons. However, during the last dive of the day it may be impossible to find such a person. In such a case, choose a diver who is in good condition and who preferably has had a shorter or shallower dive than others or ideally has had one of the first dives of the day. In the last case you may have a little difficulty getting them to kit up again. Note that Stand-by divers, though rarely used, are a major aid to safety.

Snorkel-cover

A rather unpopular task. Beware snorkel divers getting hypothermia. Note that snorkel-cover cannot do much in the case of an underwater diving accident, though they may be very useful if the accident occurs on the surface. These is a strong argument for putting them in a cover boat ready to enter the water should need arise. In this position they keep warmer, less bored and more able to observe divers on the surface than when they are face down in the water.

FINAL PLANNING

On arrival at the site the Expedition Leader notes his personnel and relates these to his earlier plans. He also notes the weather and sea conditions and any other points that may make him alter his plans.

Then quickly he or she decides how, when and whether diving will take place (see later for a discussion of when diving should be abandoned). He or she makes up the list of dives bearing in mind the need to ensure that the most experienced dive with the least experienced, that no-one spends too long on any one job, particularly if they might get cold or bored, and that an adequate number of people must be on shore (or on a boat) to run the dive. Lesser aims in this making of a dive list are:

(i) to ensure that groups of divers have roughly the same sizes of air cylinders

(ii) to ensure that divers who have the same aims dive together, and

(iii) to give effect to the aim that other things being equal, divers acquire new partners so that they widen their experience of styles of diving.

Then the Expedition Leader briefs every one, explaining who the various officers are, the general progress and aims of the expedition. A list of dives should be posted with the personnel, approximate times and effective officers for each stage of the dive listed. After all this, the dive should proceed: high time too!

DURING THE DIVE

After good planning which has been clearly explained to the members of the expedition, everything should proceed correctly. Dive groups will assemble at the right time, report to the Dive Marshal and enter the water after checking each other. Dives will finish with the dive leaders signalling to the Dive Marshal and then reporting to him or her with dive times and depths. Ideally the Expedition Leader and the Deputy Expedition Leader have only two precise functions at this stage:

1. To check that the dives are proceeding according to plan. This may involve them in giving individual officers extra help at times.

2. To watch for any change in conditions which would lead to the dive being abandoned or modified, see later. They should also check that no person is being overworked, bored or getting cold, even if the victim wants to suffer (some want to be heroic).

AFTER THE DIVE

When everyone has dived and the Expedition Leader can account for everyone, he or she completes the dive log. If the dive expedition was run for a particular purpose, or if any particular incidents took place or planned events failed to happen, the Expedition Leader will probably want to have a debriefing session at which these matters can be talked over. Often, particularly in Scotland, it is a pleasure to retire to a pub to do this, but if matters are serious, an immediate on-site discussion may be required.

Before leaving the site, the Expedition Leader checks that everyone has left the place tidy, while the Equipment Officer checks that all Branch equipment is safely in his care. The Expedition Leader may need to thank a local landowner or official for access to the shore or report to a Coastguard or Harbourmaster that they have returned safely to shore.

Later, preferably on the same day, the dive log and records made on site are used to complete a dive report, see Figs. 78a, b. The report should state who dived, to what depths, for how long, who the officers were, weather and

Fig. 77. Check-list for correct kitting-up of a diver

Dry suit	Properly fitted. No holes. Inflation mechanism operates; buddy notes inflation and deflation valve position.
Wet suit Hood, bootees Gloves	Complete. Properly zipped up. No constriction of the diver.
Life jacket	Properly fitted with harness straps in place. Drain valve/plug closed. Mouthpiece in place, hose free and unconstricted. Cylinder if fitted full with hand valve accessible. Direct-feed, if fitted, in place.
Mask	Present, fitted or ready to be fitted.
Snorkel	Straps not overloose or broken.
Fins	Buckles in place and not broken
Knife	Straps tight, restraining ring or clip around knife.
Cylinder	Cylinder tight in its binding band(s).
Backpack Harness	Harness and backpack undamaged and properly fitted, make sure that no part of the LJ is covered by the harness.
Regulator (Demand valve)	Correctly fitted to cylinder with mouthpiece right way up (exhaust ports downwards on most models). Octopus mouthpiece (if fitted) easily available but not in way of other equipment.
Contents Gauge	Working and registering full or nearly full contents. Positioned so diver can easily take hold of it to see it.
Depth Gauge Compass, Watch	Fitted securely and easy for diver to view.
Weight Belt	Securely fitted at narrowest part of trunk. Fitted on top of any LJ or cylinder harness and unobstructed for quick release. Quick release fitted and working. Weights symmetrically arranged on either side.
Function Test	Pillar valve open, check operation of regulator by breathing from it, check that there are no leaks, check cylinder pressure. Direct feeds (if fitted) operate correctly.

sea conditions, bottom conditions, tests taken (if any). This report goes into the Branch records.

ABANDONING A DIVE

Above all an Expedition Leader must be able to judge when to stop diving while still in the midst of an expedition. Situations which call for this are as follows:

1. Deterioration in the weather and sea conditions. Obviously the EL must make the decision to suspend diving before conditions become too bad to dive and he must do this in time to get divers out of the water. He or she must remember just how long it will take to get divers up and whether there is any way of speeding this up. Obviously if your divers are diving a long way off shore with the only boat, it may take a whole dive duration, plus time to recover the divers, plus time to return to shore. This can be a very difficult decision for an EL who may find it hard to estimate how fast the weather is deteriorating. For instance, a dive near shore might start in the wind shadow of a force 7 wind so that diving is perfectly safe. The wind may be backing and will eventually come to blow along and then on to the dive site. Decisions may be difficult in these conditions, but weather such as experienced in the Sound of Mull in 1977 when the wind went from force 0 to 7 in 30 minutes are unusual.

Basically, inexperienced divers cannot cope with sea states above 3 while experienced divers can cope with states up to about 5, though the wave frequency rather than height may be features which most affect divers trying to get aboard a boat or a shore. Trying to board a boat in a confused sea or with very frequent waves is much more difficult than doing this in a big sea with regular widely spaced waves. Boarding a boat is easier for a diver than coming ashore in the water though it may be that the site will have a piece of water sheltered from the sea for entry and exit in heavy seas. All divers and boat drivers should always consider where would be the best place to land before going into or on the water and they should also note its relationship to prominent landmarks because a shore looks quite different when at sea compared with its appearance from land.

2. Diminution in the number of personnel to run a dive safely. For instance if someone feels unwell, or becomes too cold while ashore, they must not take further part in the dive. If the absence of this person deprives the EL of essential or highly desirable safety features, the dive must be abandoned or suspended till personnel become available. Similarly if any member of the party is inconsiderate enough to wander off ashore or to be too slow in getting ready, you as EL may have to abandon the dive temporarily or even permanently. Running a dive with a bare minimum of trained personnel, for instance four experienced divers for ten trainees on their first or second dive, is likely to get you into a situation where the dive should be abandoned; running it with only two trained personnel would probably be impossible from the start. In such cases you should have appreciated this in your pre-dive planning and cancelled the dive; or had a joint expedition with another Branch; or invited some Instructors along.

3. Unexplained or serious illness or accident to anyone ashore or in the water. Obviously this situation will require the EL to direct first aid, rescue, and contact with local doctor, police, coastguard or recompression chamber. In addition, any diving incident and some shore incidents may well require a written report from the EL so he or she will need to take notes of what happened as soon as possible.

4. Presence of surface craft over the dive site in excessive numbers. Dives should never be made in the fairway to a port without the agreement and encouragement of the port authorities.

5. If ordered to leave the site either on land or at sea by the appropriate authorities. At the time of writing there are only a few prohibited areas in Scotland; some of these areas are prohibited to divers only at certain times.

Notes on use of Dive Report form. Complete the form during each diving expedition as it progresses.

Note on Fig. 78b that the heading 'site' is repeated for each dive. The purpose of this is that this will permit the person logging the dives to indicate slight changes in the part of the site used by each dive. It is a good idea to record the amount of air in each diver's cylinder(s) at the start of the dive. It is not so important to record the amount remaining at the end of the dive though this may be of interest. The reason for recording the amount of air they start with is that in the rare event of an accident or of a diver becoming overdue in surfacing an accurate estimate can be made of the possible duration of remaining air for the diver. This information is of value in deciding and carrying out on search and rescue dives with the stand-by divers and will be asked for if you call in the Coastguard in the event of an accident. Remember to calculate the actual amount of air in the cylinder(s) at the start of the dive by taking into account the actual pressure in the cylinders. Thus a 200 BAR cylinder filled only to 160 BAR will contain only 80% of its nominal say 72 cubic foot capacity, i.e. 57.6 cubic foot. The amount of air in a diver's set can be recorded against his or her name as in Fig. 78b. If copying this form we suggest you use an enlarging photocopier and enlarge it to 125 or 133%.

DIVE REPORT FORM

Site ....Date.......................

Expedition Leader ....

Equipment Officer ....

Safety Officer (First Aid)...

Dive Marshal..

Boat Driver(s)...

Purpose of Dive

Club Equipment on Site

Boat   Outboard   Life Jackets, No.....   Aqualung Cylinders, No........

Demand Valves   Weight Belts

Site of Nearest Recompression Facilities

Nearest Doctor

Weather   Cloud

              Wind

Sea Conditions   Sea State   Tide

                     Swell   Current

Tests Taken

U/W Conditions at Site

Fig. 78a.

Site ....Date................   Site ....Date................

Dive No. ....   Dive No. ....

Dive Leader ....   Dive Leader ....

Other Divers ....   Other Divers ....

....

....

Time in ....   Time in ....

Time out ....   Time out ....

Max. Depth ....   Max. Depth ....

Cover ....   Cover ....

Boatdriver ....   Boatdriver ....

Standby ....   Standby ....

Site ....Date................   Site ....Date................

Dive No. ....   Dive No. ....

Dive Leader ....   Dive Leader ....

Other Divers ....   Other Divers ....

....

....

Time in ....   Time in ....

Time out ....   Time out ....

Max. Depth ....   Max. Depth ....

Cover ....   Cover ....

Boatdriver ....   Boatdriver ....

Standby ....   Standby ....

Fig. 78b

Chapter 7

Boathandling and Navigation

Soon after completing pool training and venturing into the open sea, the newly fledged diver will start using boats of some sort or another, and will continue to do so for the rest of his diving career. Boats should not be taken for granted, they form a vital link in the chain of life support which includes all diving equipment. A failure of boat or engine, or a mistake in navigation or a wrong decision on the part of the boat handler can cause death as surely as equipment failure at depth.

BOATS AND BOATWORK

THE BOAT

For most divers a boat means an inflatable. Modern fabrics such as Hypalon mean that all well-known makes of inflatable are tough and reliable. There is a wide choice available, from which it is easy to eliminate the 'paddling pool' variety which is both useless and dangerous for diving or any other maritime activity. It is important that the inflatable be fitted with wooden floorboards, metal or fibreglass base, as a rubber floor will not stand the wear, and severely reduces speed. A bow dodger will be useful to prevent spray from filling the boat, whilst lifelines round the outside of the tubes will greatly assist boarding from the water. Remember that some inflatables are designed for long and some for short shaft motors, the two are not interchangeable. One of the great advantages of the inflatable is that its main tubes are usually subdivided into three or more compartments, so that if any one is damaged and leaking, the boat will survive and be navigable on the other two. These boats are easy to transport; in the boot of the car when deflated, on the roof or on a simple trailer when inflated. Beware the maker's handbook which tells you that the boat can be assembled within minutes – all of them take at least half an hour of concerted effort to assemble. They can be easily manhandled over a rocky foreshore, yet can carry a heavy load at speed.

Their capacity is limited more by space than by displacement. This means that if the sea state permits you can safely cram divers and their gear on board. For example, a 10′6″ boat with a 4′9″ beam and a main tube diameter of 14″ gives a total displacement of one ton. They are extremely stable, a plump diver with twinset can struggle aboard without couping the lot. Because the inflatable resembles a large fender, people often neglect the proper fendering precautions. It should be borne in mind that whereas your boat will ride quite happily alongside the smooth wooden hull of a parent craft, it will soon be cut to ribbons by projections or barnacles on a pier or rocks. Inflatables are designed to plane, that is to skim along the surface of the water rather than plough solidly through it. At slow speeds, off the plane, the boat will respond very sluggishly to steering. Because they sit on top of the water, inflatables are strongly influenced by the wind – try paddling one against a stiff breeze! For this reason the choice of motor is important to drive the boat satisfactorily to windward. For a 12′ boat at least a 15 hp motor. Most inflatables can be fitted with remote controls, extra seats, windscreens and possibly cocktail cabinets – don't be tempted – all this extra clutter takes up space, windscreens are easily broken, and the most obvious place to sit in an inflatable is on the tubes anyway. In heavy seas it may be prudent to crouch down in the middle, thus lowering the centre of gravity. Outboards of up to 40 hp can be controlled by a tiller with throttle twist grip, but here a word of warning. Any inflatable lightly laden and bouncing off a wavetop can be overturned should the wind get underneath. Also yanking the throttle wide open suddenly can pitch the driver out over the stern. Very amusing to watch from the shore, but also very deadly to anyone who may be in the water.

The small hardboat or conventional dinghy in wood, glassfibre, or what have you is not so attractive to divers. Whereas the normal 12′

inflatable will take four divers plus gear, a similar wooden dinghy may be dangerously overloaded with three. Again the lack of stability is a problem with divers coming and going over the side. Also it's very easy to hurt one's ribs hauling in over the side of a hard-boat. The Dory type of craft is usually the apple of its owner's eye; so it should be considering the price they are. They provide greater space than any craft size for size and are extremely stable. Their main disadvantages are hard sides, a tendency to hammer at speed, and a disconcerting habit of spooning large waves inboard.

Divers will often charter larger boats, MFV's or motor yachts, to take them further afield on more ambitious expeditions. Here it's important to remember that although you and your dive officer probably have a very fixed idea of exactly where you want to go and what you want to do, the skipper is in law 'master under God' and is responsible for your safety whilst on his boat. A little tact in your consultation with him will usually be amply repaid. Also bear in mind that all his professional training has taught him to keep well away from rocks, wrecks and other marine hazards, and here's a group of madmen wanting to be put right on them! Don't jump off a large boat without giving some thought as to how you are going to get back on again. Is there a ladder provided? If so is it one you can climb with fins and gear on – if not are there ropes provided to fasten gear to? In open water dives it is often practicable for the dive to be conducted from the parent vessel; on these occasions it is important that no one jumps in before the skipper gives word that the screw has stopped. Make sure the skipper understands what is going on and where you are likely to surface. If the parent vessel is anchored, then because of the time taken to get a large boat moving it is prudent to have an inflatable in the water manned by a standby diver and boat driver. If the parent vessel is not anchored, then it is important that it stays clear of the diving area as the skipper will need to rotate his screw from time to time to maintain station. Note that diving from an unanchored vessel presents extra hazards to divers. The depth of water may be uncertain while surfacing will be slightly risky for both divers and skippers. This mode of diving should not be used when inexperienced or trainee divers are diving. When picking up divers, the vessel should ideally stop some distance up wind and tide of the divers and stream a floating line if necessary. Skippers should not head straight for divers then stop with a sharp jab astern: it's disconcerting to see enormous bows bearing down on you, and the swirl of a large boat going astern can sweep you away from the ladder. Remember that most boats have restricted visibility under the bows; if you can't see the skipper, he certainly can't see you. In this context it is worth emphasising the importance of a good lookout being kept by the boat party. Diving can often be carried out in open water with fairly heavy seas running; on surfacing only about 18″ of a diver shows above the surface: not really very much if there are 5′ waves.

A checklist of equipment to be carried in a boat is given in Fig. 79.

Fig. 79. A check-list of the equipment that should be carried on a small dive-boat.

FOR ALL TRIPS
Anchor (Meon or Admiralty types are probably best)
Chain
Warp (rope) for anchor, say 40 metres
Bailer
2 or better 3 paddles or oars
Flares in waterproof box
　　Orange smoke for daytime
　　Red light parachute flare for night
Foot-pump (inflatables only)
Knife on lanyard
First Aid kit in waterproof box
Spares and tools for engine
　　(Spare plugs, plugspanner, spanner and screwdriver to take recoil cover off outboard, shear pins (if needed for propellor), pliers, spare propellor)
Small buoy
2 × 25 metre light lines
Compass
Diving flag and support pole

FOR LONGER TRIPS (say 1 hour or more trip time) add
Spare fuel
Drinking water
Small supply of food, say chocolate
Hot drink in thermos
Torch
Chart in waterproof cover

Boathandling

Most divers get their introduction to boatwork in the club inflatable. The idea that anyone can jump in and drive off is untrue and unsafe: ideally only personnel trained in boathandling should be allowed to drive. Particular attention should be paid to the boat's equipment before setting off. Is there sufficient fuel of the right mixture with an adequate safety margin for the trip? Are the oars or paddles there? Are they the right ones for the boat and are they in good order? Even if you don't intend anchoring there should be an anchor with a short length of chain and sufficient rope – give some thought as to how you will secure the anchor line to the boat, and make sure you do before heaving the anchor over. You should also have onboard compass, bellows, repair kit for inflatable, spare plugs and spanner together with shearpins and split pins for the motor.

If you are broken down and being carried rapidly out to sea and away from your frantically gesticulating divers, you will be glad of some means of attracting attention. The ideal article is the small flare marketed specially for divers which has a yellow smoke signal for daylight use in one end, and a red locating flare in the other. If all else fails remember the internationally recognised distress signal of slowly raising and lowering the arms from shoulder height; S.O.S. flashed on a torch, an item of clothing waved from an oar paddle, or, obviously enough, flames from any part of the boat. Remember that H.M. Coastguard are the co-ordinating authority for all air/sea rescue operations. Before setting out make sure someone ashore knows your estimated time of return and knows how to contact the Coastguard (by dialling 999) should you be overdue. You can also file a plan of your expedition with the Coastguard who will then pull the panic switch if you don't report back on time. Nimrods and helicopters scouring the West Coast of Scotland while you down a pint in the MacDonald Arms would not do the diving image a lot of good; so it's important that this facility is treated responsibly.

Once at sea, remember that running at slightly less than full throttle will use much less fuel than if you run full throttle all the way. Also there will be a comfortable speed to suit the prevailing sea conditions. Avoid travelling at 'hump speed' when the boat is not quite planing – use full throttle to get on the plane then ease back a little for economic running.

You can make life easier by going at an angle to the waves rather than crashing straight over them. Apart from possible damage to the stringers of the boat or to loose gear onboard, the people sitting nearer the bows are probably having a more uncomfortable ride than you are, and in extreme cases could suffer spinal damage. A high speed boat in unskilled hands is as lethal as a car. As the boat driver, you can be held responsible for any injury or damage caused to anybody or anything which your boat may come into contact with, so keep a good lookout, or if you can't see over the forest of snorkels in the boat with you ask someone in front to keep an eye ahead. Your outboard propellor is potentially lethal to people in the water; don't drive near swimmers, or allow divers to approach the boat until the screw is stopped. On motors fitted with gears, should there be any doubt at all as to where the neutral position is, switch off. Don't tow divers or anyone else from the lifeline round the boat, if they loose their grip they are right in the propeller; if you want to tow, use a long line astern. Remember than an inflatable laden with divers and gear makes quite a wash even when travelling slowly, do all you can to minimise the wash when passing near other boats or swimmers. Driving a fast inflatable is like operating any other high speed machinery, you have to concentrate. Always carry flag alpha and see it is prominently displayed when divers are down. The inflatable should never be left unattended when divers are down; the anchor could drag, moreover inflatables are notoriously short of solid places to tie an anchor to, the D ring at the bow may well have been weakened by towing and does on occasions pull out.

The outboard motor

Whether you have a reliable, trouble free machine, or one which will let you down at every opportunity depends on you: how you service your motor, how you fuel and operate it, and how you lay it up in the off season. Considering the outboard motor spends its working life running at maximum revolutions in a hostile environment of sea, air and spray it is remarkable that they work at all. Always stick to the manufacturers' recommendations regarding fuel mixture, and be punctilious about mixing and storing the fuel, using a filter funnel at every opportunity. Many outboard troubles arise through contaminated or wrongly mixed fuel so it's worth taking a bit of trouble here. The drive from engine to propellor is often fitted with a shearpin at the propellor, this pin will break should the propellor strike anything thus saving damage to the gearing or motor. Even if you keep clear of rocks, the pin could shear on contact with a piece of driftwood or a thick chunk of seaweed, so always carry several spare shearpins, with retaining splitpins and pliers. Should the propellor be damaged, you can seriously damage the motor by continuing to operate at high speeds because of the vibrations set up. Unlike the old motors, which would run after being dropped in the sea, and which could be stripped down in the boat, the modern outboard is a sophisticated piece of machinery, which needs to be serviced by experts. Anything more than a change of plugs or a blocked fuel line and you may as well forget about it. Always carry spare plugs, and spare fuel filter where applicable. If your motor does not start after half a dozen pulls, something is wrong and to continue pulling will only make it worse. It may be as simple as no fuel or a flooded carburettor, get your breath back and look round before trying again. In order to get the most out of your outboard motor, it is essential to ensure that it is mounted correctly. Immediately above the propellor you will see the cavitation plate, this is to prevent air being drawn into the propellor, and should be level with the bottom of the boat, or marginally below it. This height can be altered by adding a fillet of wood to the transome, or by shaving it down. The cavitation plate should be parallel to the boat's bottom. As a rough guide to fuel consumption, at just below full throttle an outboard will consume about one pint of fuel per horsepower/hour. A substantial saving can be made by operating at slower speeds as outlined above.

Speed through the water

It is useful to have an accurate knowledge of your speed through the water – this should be particularly clear from reading the next section on 'Navigation'. Unfortunately it is very hard to assess your speed in the diver's favourite craft, the inflatable, unless you can time your movement from one point to another whose distance apart can be read on a chart. Unfortunately the speed of an inflatable is markedly affected by loading and by sea con-

ditions. A planing inflatable might be running at 20-25 knots while the same boat wallowing heavily laden might make only 5 knots through the water. On larger boats of the types that might be used by divers, patent logs, which measure the number of revolutions of a small towed propellor, are useful. The patent logs register the number of revolutions as miles or parts of a mile through the water and this information can be used to calculate speed though of course distance through the water is generally the most useful measurement. At low speeds the crude method, termed the Dutchman's log, can be used. A small floating object is thrown ahead of the bows and the time at which stem and then the time at which the stern passes the object are noted. If you know the length of the boat the speed can be calculated. Don't forget that speed through the water is just that, it is not the speed over the bottom unless there is no current. 6 kt through the water when the current is setting against you at 2 kt is only 4 kt effective.

NAVIGATION

Navigation is commonly regarded as a black art which can only be practised by those versed in spherical trigonometry. This is not so, for the principles of coastal navigation are well within the grasp of anyone capable of passing the 3rd Class lecture examination. The first requirement of the navigator is, usually, to get to B from A without getting lost and in as short a time as possible. If you can see B when you set out from A there may be little problem, but if B is out of sight by reason of distance or poor visibility then a problem exists – we need to know a course to steer.

In full the aims of navigation are:

To find out where your are.

To find out where you want to sail to.

To find the best route to your destination.

To check that you are following your route and to be able to work out appropriate corrections should you find that you have strayed from that course.

The best route is sometimes one which requires some subtlety. Obviously you don't want your route to take you across areas that might be too shallow for the draught of your boat at the stage of the tide you are making your trip. You want to choose the fastest course. This may not be the one which is the shortest on the chart because current or wind may slow you down and lead to an inordinate expenditure of time and fuel. If you have the choice of two or more launching sites navigation methods will allow you to decide which will give you the shortest trip time. The answer is not necessarily that the nearest launching point is the best. At some states of tide the current will flow against you on the way out and again on the way back a few hours later when you use one launching site whereas one placed differently may give you the aid of the current both ways. On other days the different times and height of the tides might alter the timing and extent of the currents in such a way that your choice of launching sites might be changed.

Very simple navigation requires four facilities:

The ability to mark a course on a chart from your starting point to your goal and to read off the bearing of this course, i.e. the direction in relation to True (T) or Magnetic (M) North.

The ability to use a compass on board boat so that you steer this course.

The ability to have worked out a set of bearings from the chart that will enable you to identify the spot, if it is in the sea, at which you intend to dive.

The ability to recognise when you've reached the point indicated by the bearings.

The equipment you need for coastal navigation is as follows:

Charts of the area, preferably at 1:10,000 or 1:25,000 scale.
The Admiralty Pilot Book for the area.
Reid's Nautical Almanack.
A parallel ruler.
A compass for steering.
A compass for taking hand bearings.
A pair of dividers.
A pencil and soft rubber.

All the above can be obtained from Admiralty Chart Agents, such as Kelvin-Hughes, 38 West George Street, Glasgow. You will also find it very useful to have a book on coastal navigation such as *Sea Navigation* by E. S. Gates, published by Harrap, or *Coastwise Navigation* by G. G. Watkins, published by Kandy Publications.

Very simple navigation

The course to steer is obtained from the chart which has on it a *Compass rose,* a circle graduated 0-360 degrees, which on Admiralty charts is always aligned North up. Lay the parallel rule along the course to be taken, draw the course on the chart, then keeping the rule parallel, run it on its rollers so that it cuts the centre of the compass rose, read off the true course.

A word here about true and magnetic courses. The magnetic north pole is different to the true north pole, moreover this amount varies from year to year and from place to place on the earth's surface; this difference is known as *variation*. The needle of the magnetic compass points to magnetic north, so we need to know the magnetic or compass course as opposed to the true course. Admiralty charts obligingly print a magnetic compass rose inside the true one, but bear in mind that this is valid only for the year of publication, due to the annual change. Another and more accurate way to obtain the compass course is to take the true course, then apply the variation, adding if west, subtracting if east. Thus a true course of 010° with a variation of 012W becomes 022°. There are various catchphrases to help remember this rule, the best is probably *Compass to true add East*, known as the Cadet rule; obviously the reverse is *True to compass, add West*. So now we have the magnetic or compass course, and can write this in large figures alongside the line drawn on the chart.

When you come to steer this course you will find it reasonably easy to keep the boat on the right bearing if you are steering a reasonably large boat with a fixed compass by the steering wheel. It is much harder to steer a course in a small hard boat or an inflatable. If you are using such craft it may be possible to sight a prominent landmark or even better two landmarks in line (transit bearing, see below) with your course, one behind the other, before you start. If you can do this following the course from landmarks lined up with a hand compass from the shore before setting out, steering will be relatively easy. Obviously if landmarks are poor or absent, or if your course has two or more legs, this is not going to work. Note however that you may be able to use landmarks on the reverse bearing, behind you. If you use a hand compass in an inflatable you'll be doing well if you can take a bearing with an accuracy of ±5° and you'll be still less accurate if you try to steer to this. In this section we are assuming that there is no effect of wind, waves or current on your progress. Methods of dealing with these effects are described later.

Position fixing to check that you arrived at the place you want to be is simply done either by transit or compass bearings or by a combination of them. The most often used is the three point fix, where bearings are taken of three or more objects on the shore which are also marked on the chart, see Fig. 80. Where the three position lines cross is your position, to be marked by a dot within a circle and the time to distinguish it from the dead reckoning position mark. In practice the line will rarely if ever at all cross at the same place, the resulting triangle is known as a 'cocked hat' and your position should always be the point in the triangle which is nearest danger. A useful position line can be taken from two shore objects in transit, a particularly useful method in an inflatable when charts etc are unlikely to be to hand. Remember that a position line only tells you part of the story, you are somewhere along its length; another position line narrows the area of possibility, the third should clinch the argument, any more should confirm it. Beware the error of trying to 'fiddle' the fix to fit in with where you think you ought to be.

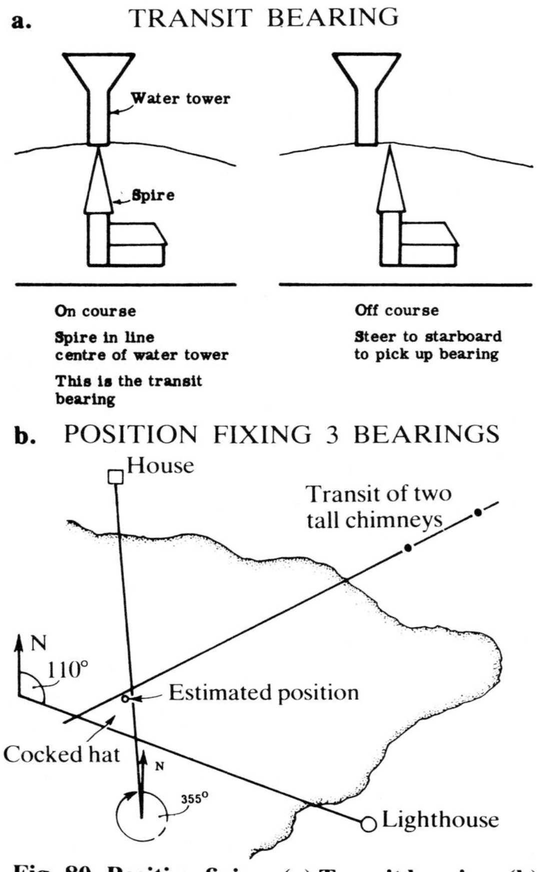

a.   TRANSIT BEARING

On course
Spire in line
centre of water tower
This is the transit
bearing

Off course
Steer to starboard
to pick up bearing

b.   POSITION FIXING 3 BEARINGS

Fig. 80. Position fixing. (a) Transit bearing. (b) Map illustrating a three point fix using two compass bearings and one transit bearing.

How long is the voyage going to take? You will have noticed that there are divisions both on the side and bottom margins of your chart, and that those on the bottom are much smaller than those on the sides. The ones on the side are minutes and degrees of latitude, and by a happy chance one minute of latitude equals one nautical mile. The ones along the bottom only equal one nautical mile at the equator and because of the distortion inherent in making the round world into a series of rectangular charts, they are not to be used for measuring distance. Because of this distortion factor, when measuring distance, always prick it off with the dividers on the latitude. Knowing the speed of your craft, prick off an hour or a half hour's run on the chart and make a note of the time you should be there. This is known as the *dead reckoning*, and is an intelligent guess of where you should be if you have steered a straight course and have not been offset by wind, waves or tide.

More advanced navigation

So far we have assumed that there are no tidal currents or effects of wind on the course you actually follow in the water, i.e. the course made good. We are also going to cover slightly more advanced methods of position fixing.

Tides

Tides not only rise and fall, but in doing so create horizontal movements in the sea. In general terms a flood or rising tide moves clockwise round the British Isles and vice versa on the ebb. Consequently, off the West Coast of Scotland the tides will generally run in a north direction when flooding and a southerly direction when ebbing. Normally there are two complete tidal cycles, two highs and two lows, in any 24 hour period, each tide being approximately 45 minutes later than the previous one. Tides are caused by the gravitational effect of the moon moving round the earth, the biggest tides occurring when both sun and moon are in conjunction on one side of the earth (see Fig. 81). These are known as spring tides – the highest highs and the lowest lows – but note that they have no connection with the spring season, occuring every fortnight (Fig. 82). The intermediate tides are known as 'Neaps' – the highest low, and the lowest high, in other words the smallest range. Tidal information can be obtained from a Nautical Almanack such as Reids which will give the times of high water at standard ports with the corrections or constants for other ports. It also gives the height of water at high water from which one can interpolate for different stages of the tide. It is important to note that the height of tide can be influenced by strong winds and by barometric pressure. Sea level falls by 10cm for every 12 millibar increase in pressure and rises similarly for a fall in barometric pressure.

Tides

Further details on the use of tide tables are given at the end of this chapter. On Admiralty charts there are a host of abbreviations and symbols – these are explained in any good nautical Almanack such as Reids, or in a special booklet obtainable from the Chart Agent (5011). Make sure you understand the difference between the symbol for a rock which shows at all states of the tide, a rock which only uncovers at low water, and one which never uncovers but is considered dangerous. All depths on the chart are reduced to chart datum, a hypothetical level below which the tide never falls, so the depths recorded there are lower than you will ever encounter, your

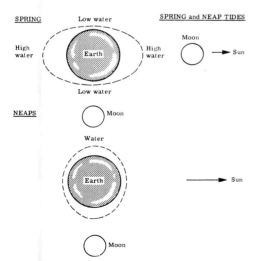

Fig. 81. Tides. Explanation of spring and neap tides.

tidal depths can be added to the charted depth (an important consideration when planning decompression stops). (Fig. 82).

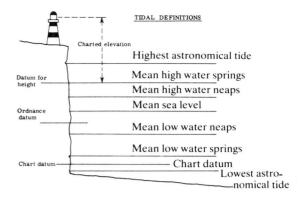

Fig. 82. Tidal definitions.

Currents and their effects

Of great interest to divers is the horizontal tidal movement. It is wrong to assume that the current is flowing in a given direction during the whole period up to the time of high water by the shore; the momentum of this vast body of water as well as topographical features mean that the time of high water by the shore is only a datum from which the speed and direction of the current can be computed. On Admiralty charts there is usually some form of tidal information. Small letters in coloured diamonds refer to a scale where the speed and direction of the current can be deduced from the time of high water at the local standard port. These values are only approximate, and are affected by weather as stated above. A strong southwesterly blowing for two or three days could affect the height of tide by several feet, and increase the horizontal current proportionately. Remember that you will be diving in many places for which there is no accurate tidal information. Your observation that slack water high at the *Rondo* wreck in the Sound of Mull is one hour and a half after HW Oban is of great practical value and deserves to be written down in your new large diving logbook.

If you are underway in a boat in a current your movement will be affected. If the current runs directly against your direction you will simply be retarded. For example if you make 5 knots through still water and the current flows at 3 knots your effective speed becomes 2 knots. Conversely, if the current is running exactly on the same bearing as your steering your progress is accelerated. If the current

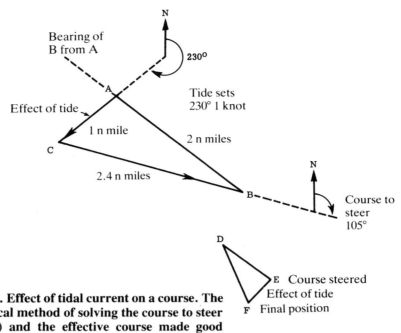

Fig. 83. Effect of tidal current on a course. The graphical method of solving the course to steer (upper) and the effective course made good (lower small triangle). See text for fuller description.

runs in any other direction both your speed and your effective course made good will be altered. In Fig. 83 we show a method of calculating graphically the course you should steer to get to your destination if a current modifies your progress. AB is the course you would steer from A to B in the absence of any current. AC is plotted with the correct bearing to indicate the direction of the current (taken from the tables on the chart and applying to the state of tide at which you are sailing). The length of AC corresponds to 1 sea mile because the current is flowing at 1 knot. The line CB gives the direction you must steer from A to reach B while affected by the current. The length of CB gives the effective distance you will have to cover and if you know your speed through still water you can now calculate how long it will take to reach B from A. Conversely, if you have steered on a particular bearing for a given time and want to estimate where you are as a result of the current, the method can be used as in the smaller diagram where DE is the course you steered, EF is the direction and distance covered by the current in that time, and DF gives your true course and distance covered.

More advanced position fixing

Earlier in this chapter we described position fixing using three transit or compass bearings to clearly visible objects on shore. Ideally these three objects should be about 120° apart. Where there are not three objects visible, one or more position lines can be transferred along the course and speed made good on the chart to provide a reasonable fix in conjunction with a single new position line. This is the transferred position line fix, Fig. 84. At 1300 hours the lighthouse on shore bore 020° (T). It was the only prominent object visible at that time. Therefore the boat's position lies somewhere on the bearing to the light. At 1400 hours the boat steering a course 100°(T) at 6 knots will be 6 nautical miles further on. Now the same light bears 315°(T). The transferred position line is laid off on the chart parallel to the 1300 hours bearing at a distance from it corresponding to 6 nautical miles. Plot the bearing at 1400 hours. The point where the transferred position and second bearing coincide gives a fix for the position at 1400 hours. This method is also known as the running fix method. For those in larger vessels and lucky enough to have access to a sextant, use can be made of the vertical sextant angle by which the distance of a known object can be calculated then combined with a visual bearing to give a satisfactory fix. The principle of this is that knowing the length of one side of a triangle, and the value of one of its angles, we can calculate the length of the other. We choose a lighthouse or other landmark whose height is given on the chart, with the sextant measure the angle between it and sea level, and calculate, or look up the convenient table, in Reid's, to get the distance off, see Fig. 85. Horizontal sextant angles can also supply useful information since they provide accurate measurement of the angle between two bearings and can be used to obtain accurate position fixes, particularly from stationary boats.

Bear in mind that some boats used by divers are equipped with Decca or Satellite position fixing equipment and that Radar can also be used for range and direction to a prominent radar reflector to establish position. Echo sounders can also be used to confirm whether the depth is consistent with your supposed position.

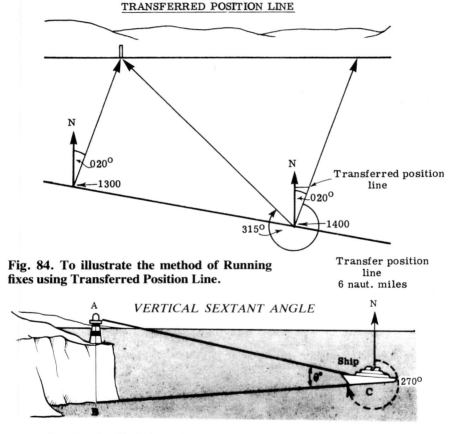

TRANSFERRED POSITION LINE

Fig. 84. To illustrate the method of Running fixes using Transferred Position Line.

Transfer position line
6 naut. miles

VERTICAL SEXTANT ANGLE

AB = Height of light from chart
Calculate distance off by formula BC = BA cot θ *or*
by tables in Reid's Almanac
Take bearing of lt. = 270°T
Range and bearing give a perfect fix

Fig. 85. Position fixing by using the Vertical Sextant Angle and bearing of an object of known height.

Having fixed our position by one or other of the above methods, we will observe that we are some distance from our dead reckoning position. From this we can plot what wind and tide have done to the ship over the period under consideration, and by reversing the triangle thus formed can obtain the course to steer, the correction, necessary to arrive at our destination.

Practical considerations

So how does all this work out in practice? No one in their right mind is going to go crashing off in the club inflatable with a chart spread on their knees, brandishing an expensive sextant, whilst parallel rulers, hand bearing compasses and other expensive items slosh about on the floorboards. The answer is that many of the skills discussed above can only reasonably be carried out on larger vessels, and their value to the inflatable borne diving expedition lies in the pre-dive planning. With the chart spread on your living room floor, plot the course to steer, magnetic, to that fabulous wreck site. Or if just going up the coast and back, plot a course to steer in case the surface viz turns nasty. It is always good news for divers to know what the tide is doing, and what it is likely to do during the course of the dive. Remember that in an inflatable compass readings are going to be only approximate, keep the compass as far as possible from steel cylinders or motor, slow down or stop the boat if necessary whilst you try to average out the swing. A small prismatic marching compass will be found more accurate for taking bearings than a diving compass. It's worth putting in a bit of practice in your inflatable under good conditions to find out what your margin of error is likely to be.

*Buoyage**

The I.A.L.A. combined Cardinal and Lateral buoyage system 'A' can best be described as follows.

Lateral Marks

Main channels into ports will be marked by red can buoys to port and green conical buoys to starboard as a vessel *enters* a harbour. The

* Department of Trade booklet *Seaway Code*. p.18-19. (Available free from H.M. Coastguard.)

situation will obviously reverse on departure. Lights exhibited will be red and green respectively.

Cardinal Marks

These are pillar shaped and will be aligned in a North, South, East and Westerly direction around an area of danger. Normally only one buoy of the four can be seen. These buoys are coloured yellow and black and exhibit white lights in known combinations of very quick flashing (120 per minute) and long flashing (at least two seconds) colour and light combinations alter depending in which quadrant the buoy lies but the most noticeable alteration to each buoy in daylight hours is its topmark. This takes the form of two black conical cones.

In the Northern quadrant the points face North. ▲ ▲

In the Southern quadrant the points face South. ▼ ▼

In the Western quadrant the points face Inwards. ▼ ▲

In the Eastern quadrant the points face Outwards. ▲ ▼

Other buoys in the IALA system 'A' are. Isolated *DANGER* marks which are red and black, pillar shaped; *SAFE* water marks coloured red and white and either spherical or pillar shaped; and *special* marks which are yellow and may be any shape.

Using tide tables

Tide tables give you the times of high and low water and the level of water above chart datum at these times for Standard ports for each day in the year. Tables of Secondary ports give the approximate times which must be added or subtracted from the tide tables of a nearby (not necessarily the nearest) standard port to get the time of high and perhaps also of low water at the secondary ports. These tables usually give details of the depth of water which must be added or subtracted from the depths given for the standard port in order to get an estimate of water depth for a secondary port. This is the way tide tables appear in nautical almanacks. The Admiralty tide tables provide

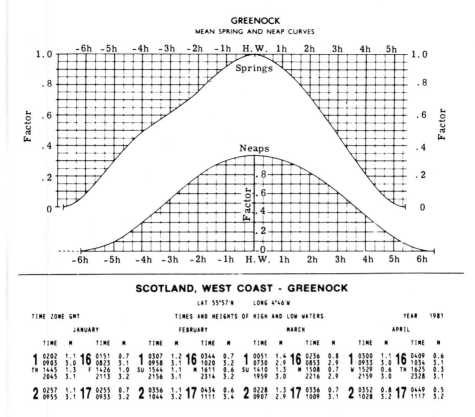

GREENOCK

MEAN SPRING AND NEAP CURVES

SCOTLAND, WEST COAST - GREENOCK

LAT 55°57'N   LONG 4°46'W

TIME ZONE GMT			TIMES AND HEIGHTS OF HIGH AND LOW WATERS								YEAR 1981
JANUARY			FEBRUARY			MARCH			APRIL		
TIME	M	TIME	M	TIME	M	TIME	M	TIME	M	TIME	M
1 0202 0903 TH 1445 2045	1.1 3.0 1.3 3.1	**16** 0151 0823 F 1426 2113	0.7 3.1 1.0 3.2	**1** 0307 0958 SU 1544 2156	1.2 3.1 1.1 3.1	**16** 0344 1020 M 1611 2314	0.7 3.2 0.6 3.2	**1** 0051 0730 SU 1410 1959	1.4 2.9 1.3 3.0	**16** 0236 0853 M 1508 2216	0.8 2.9 0.7 2.9	**1** 0300 0933 W 1529 2159	1.1 3.0 0.6 3.0	**16** 0409 1034 TH 1625 2328	0.6 3.1 0.3 3.1
2 0257 0955	1.1 3.1	**17** 0255 0933	0.7 3.2	**2** 0356 1044	1.1 3.2	**17** 0434 1111	0.6 3.4	**2** 0228 0907	1.3 2.9	**17** 0336 1009	0.7 3.1	**2** 0352 1028	0.8 3.2	**17** 0449 1117	0.5 3.2

Fig. 86a. A standard curve for the tidal rise and fall at a Standard Port, e.g. Greenock. Note the plot is of the factor value for a certain time before or after local high water, 86b, an extract from the tables for 1981 for Greenock showing the information supplied, note that the tables give the times of successive high and low waters and the height of these above chart datum in metres. *Reproduced from a portion of the British Admiralty Tide Tables with the sanction of the Controller, HM Stationery Office and the Hydrographer of the Navy.*

these same details but add curves for the actual rise and fall of water at each standard port so that the reader can obtain a very accurate estimate of the depth of water at any state of the tide. These standard curves give the rise as a factor (fraction) of the full tidal range for each 20 minutes of the period between low water and the next. Separate curves are given for spring and neap tides. If your tide is a spring or a neap you simply note the time you are interested in and read off the appropriate factor in terms of time before or after high water. See Fig. 86. Then you multiply the range for the day by that factor to get the depth of water above chart datum. If you want to find the time at which you will have a particular depth of tide you can calculate the factor that corresponds to the depth of water you want as a fraction of the total tidal rise for that day, see main table, you then read off the appropriate time from the factor using the standard curve.

If you are estimating rise at a given time or time for a given rise at a tide between neap and springs, estimate separately from both the spring and neap curves and average the result. Times or extent of rise at secondary ports are rather more complex and less accurate in estimation and slightly more difficult to compute. We refer you to the instructions in the Admiralty tide tables.

(Chapter 7 was written by Bruce Howard with the buoyage section by Hugh McLean.)

Chapter 8

Advanced diving

WRECK DIVING

Preliminary Research

Wreck research can start from any one of three angles. The first is set in motion by a diver locating a wreck by chance and wanting to know more about how and when it happened. A logbook entry of the type 'dived about 1 mile west of Kilmory and close inshore jammed in a rock crevice is the remains of a steel hull between 60 and 80 foot long. Must try and get more details' is the starting place for this type of research. The second type is more general, starting from a wish to know about all the wrecks that have occurred in a specific area. For example, this may be initiated by the BDO announcing 'the branch outing this summer will be to Islay. Does anyone know any good sites there?' The object of this research is to obtain information for as many wrecks as possible so that as many potential wreck sites are known before the expedition begins. The third and final type of quest is the tracing of information on a specific ship, without at first knowing its actual site, so that the amount of underwater searching is reduced.

The first type of search 'what have I found?' can be the hardest. Obviously vessels lost as a result of foundering or collision are more likely to sink intact, whereas a stranded vessel will have been pounded to pieces by sea action. The diver visiting a wreck in deeper water will be rewarded with being able to obtain accurate sizes, or establish whether it was sail or steam, screw or paddle. A widely dispersed pile of scrap has to be searched very diligently for the smallest clue. If you are lucky enough to find objects that have been ignored or missed by previous salvors, e.g. pottery, armament or even something as apparently mundane as a winch gear manufacturer's nameplate then you have a valuable clue which may require expert knowledge from any one of hundreds of fields if you are to identify and date the wreck.

Do not forget that anything removed from a wreck in UK waters must be left with the local Receiver of Wrecks. There are complex laws, based originally on the Merchant Shipping Act of 1898, relating to salvage and to the disposal of an unclaimed wreck. If you wish to salve items from a wreck and to retain an interest in these items obtain legal advice. Remember that a wreck belongs to someone and that you will have to obtain permission or a licence to salve from a wreck, or buy the wreck from the owner. The owner is often an insurance company who when traced may be prepared to sell you the wreck for a small sum. If the wreck appears to be pre-XIXth century you would be performing a public service by reporting its existence to such bodies as the Institute of Marine Archaeology, St Andrews University.

The Wrecks Section of the Hydrographic Department at Taunton, Somerset is the first place to ask if you are identifying a wreck. There is a search fee which is based on the amount of work involved in answering your query but this may be reduced or waived if you can provide them with information. They produce a booklet *Wreck Information* describing their services and containing other useful information.

'Local knowledge' is of particular importance in wreck research. However be warned that this sort of information may not be strictly accurate, having been in many cases handed down by word of mouth. Take for example two such pieces of local folklore. The first relates to a wreck found north of Portpatrick in Galloway, locally supposed to be of a boat called the *O'Ryan*. This would seem to be a plausible name until you find that you cannot trace such a vessel but realise that the site is less than a mile from the resting place of the *Orion*. The *Orion* was wrecked in 1850 with considerable loss of life, and it is possible that, over the years, the name has been corrupted. Does the *O'Ryan* wreck really have a separate existence, and if so what is its real name? The second 'almost right' case concerns the *Doris* lost according to contemporary newspapers on 12th July 1909 at Neist Point, Skye. But the Black Museum near Colbost has a handwritten note on the wall about the *Doric* being wrecked at Neist Point at the turn of the century. If you refer to Lloyds Register of Ships for 1909 and that for 1910 you will find that the *Doris* was withdrawn from the register in 1910 but that there is no record of the name *Doric* at all. This short story underlines the point that local information must always be confirmed by documentary evidence.

If however the Hydrographic Department cannot provide information and local inhabitants cannot provide rumour you probably have a large amount of work ahead. So you move to the second type of enquiry, namely to find out what wrecks are believed to be in a certain area, hoping that you can identify your wreck from amongst those on the list. The only solution is to read of and note all wrecks in the area of interest and compare your own find with each possible alternative. Of course you may start by doing this just to find out if there is anything interesting about.

The following sources of information should be used:

1. Details of all the wrecks in a certain area that are known to the Hydrographic Department can be obtained from them for a price. This list is unlikely to contain pre-1914 wrecks, unless they were or are navigational hazards, or of stranded wrecks which were not navigational hazards. Unfortunately divers are often interested in wrecks which originally were strandings since these are more likely to be accessible to divers than those which sank far offshore.

2. The Parliamentary Papers from 1852 to 1918 contain an annual list of shipping losses. These papers are available in certain libraries such as the National Library of Scotland in Edinburgh, the Mitchell and Glasgow University Libraries in Glasgow, and access can be obtained, usually by written application to the Librarian. These lists provide the basic details of many hundreds of wrecks.

3. Lloyds List was published as a broadsheet from 1741 giving general shipping news. It is a source of wreck information for the period before 1852 but locations are not accurate being of the 'in Orkney' type.

4. Old and local newspapers are another valuable source of information. Since wrecks tend to be of most interest locally local news-

papers tend to be of more value than national papers. Many of the larger public libraries carry sets of the older papers.

5. Letters to the Editors of diving magazines asking for information often lead to useful information.

6. Do not forget to note vessels posted as missing when you read old papers for these boats may have had to pass your search area and perhaps sank there.

7. Finally you may find valuable or incidental information in all manner of surprising places. For instance the photograph of Tantallon Castle in the *Times* for 17th September 1927 just happens to show the wreck of the *Elterwater* in the background. Or again for instance, the book *Tales and traditions of the Lews* by D. MacDonald contains stories about the island of Lewis. One of these relates the wrecking of a large unknown vessel in 1775. The book states 'she was loaded with iron ... hence the sunken rock which caused such a metallic sounding crash is called "Bogha an Iaruinn" and the sharp fangs of rock off Carnish Point upon which she was beaten to pieces belongs to the Sgeir an Iaruinn'. This illustrates the way in which sites can acquire a name from an event such as a shipwreck. The rock called 'The Merchant' off the west coast of Skye records the wrecking of the *Chadwick* which was carrying a general cargo. A final example of the value of unlikely sources comes from a close reading of the *Times* in 1844 which noted the dedication of a monument on the island of Deerness. The monument commemorates the loss of a Covenanter ship in 1679. Enquiry of the Scottish Covenanter Memorials Association revealed that the event commemorated was the wrecking of the *Crown* at Scarva Taing on 10th December 1679 whilst en route from Leith to America.

The third type of wreck research is in theory the simplest, namely the tracing of information on a specific named vessel. If you know the name and the approximate date of loss you should approach the following bodies for information: the Wreck Section of the Hydrographic Department, the Department of Trade (successor to the Board of Trade), Trinity House, Lloyds, the Committee for Nautical Archaeology and the Salvage Association. In addition it may be worth using the index for the *Times* (1785 onwards) or that for the *Glasgow Herald* (1906 to 1968).

To sum up, wreck research is a long involved process.

Searching underwater for a wreck

A great many problems have still to be solved when we actually come to dive on a wreck site. Are we diving on a site no one has visited before or are we visiting a well known one? Let us take the problems associated with the unknown site first.

It is extremely unlikely that you will be able to go out in a boat, throw the anchor over the side and dive right on top of your unknown though thoroughly researched wreck. Once you have established an approximate position for your wreck from your researches you will have to develop a search system. The following factors should be borne in mind:

(i) Depth of water; (ii) seabed topography; (iii) prevailing surface conditions; (iv) average water clarity; (v) site exposure; (vi) site accessibility; (vii) search area extent; (viii) type(s) of equipment available; (ix) numbers and skills of divers available; (x) time available and (xi) probable costs and funds available.

Sad to say ships usually fail to sink in easily accessible, sheltered locations so most of the problems listed above will be appreciable ones calling for expert planning and skilled diving.

Search patterns will need to be devised and adapted from the standard ones and equipment such as echo sounders, compasses, sextants, ropes, buoys, weights, metal detectors and boats will be needed. Perseverance and expert boat-handling will almost certainly be called for. If the wreck is badly broken up or corroded or spread over a large area surface search methods may miss the wreck so that there is nothing for it but to start to search underwater. You may feel that getting underwater is the whole or at least an important object of the exercise but we would put it to you that you should do as much preliminary research and surface searching as possible before diving. The reason is that once underwater you subject yourself to a slower method of search in which it is harder to plot what areas you have and have not searched and which is fraught with problems such as hypothermia of divers, possible decompression requirements etc.

The following methods can be used in searching from the surface.

1. Towing a grapnel anchor until it snags on something. Then diving to check its catch. The grapnel should if possible be towed a suitable distance above the sea bed so that it only catches objects of the size (or larger) that you expect. This is a slow method with many disappointments. Drag lines or warps may also be used.

2. Making a series of runs with a recording echosounder running. If you are able to plot your successive runs over the area you can form a good idea of the position of anything that looks like a wreck on the echosounder. Unfortunately wrecks may not appear as silhouettes of ships on the recorder and sometimes rocks give ship-like echos.

3. A towed proton magnetometer will detect large ferrous metal wrecks by the distortion they cause in the magnetic field. A fairly expensive device which is just about within the financial range of diving branches.

4. Using side scan sonar. This special type of sonar is far too expensive for a sub-aqua club but you might be lucky enough to have temporary access to the use of a vessel equipped with this equipment which gives a 'good' picture of the seabed.

Methods 2, 3 and 4 require expert navigation and even Method 1 benefits a lot from expert navigation.

5. If the water is clear or shallow, aerial observation and photography may be very valuable as a search method.

If you have found your wreck, or even another one you did not know about, you should buoy it immediately and establish its position as accurately as possible. Bearings to appropriate marks (see Ch. 7) are useful but horizontal sextant angle charts or/and Decca co-ordinates will if you use them, be far more accurate. Again you may be given details of a wreck site in terms of bearings etc. or even soundings and these should be used in finding it again.

Underwater search methods

Sweep searches and snag line searches are fully described in the Introductory Manual. They cover relatively small areas so that if a series of searches of either of these two types is needed carefully surveying and marking of the position of each search on a chart is needed to ensure that coverage is complete but not needlessly repetitive. The snag-line search can be developed into a swim-line search in which a number of divers is spread out along the line. The precise technique of doing this is set out in BSAC Paper No. 2.

In the aquaplane search a diver is towed along above the bottom on an aquaplane. The boat driver drives fairly slowly on a very accurate course maintained if possible by good transit bearings on land. The diver will become rapidly tired in the arms unless a well designed aquaplane with seat and foot holds is used. The diver carries a small marker buoy with him. If he sights the wreck or anything interesting he leaves the aquaplane, fastens the buoy to the wreck and surfaces up the buoy line. Large search areas can be covered rapidly but the effectiveness of search depends on the accuracy of navigation. You should also bear in mind that the diver dives alone even though he can use the buoy and release it in emergency. A powerful motor is needed to pull the aquaplane.

Diving on and in wrecks

What do you do once you have found the wreck? If it is a relatively modern wreck you will probably simply want to look round, and perhaps take photographs. If it is an historic wreck and you have spent a great deal of time on preliminary research and then on surface or underwater search you may well have decided already to report it as a site of possible archaeological interest for further investigation under professional guidance and maybe legal protection. If there is any possibility that your wreck is of this type be most careful while diving to prevent damage or disturbance to the site. The correct approach is to avoid any disturbance to the site and to consult a marine archaeologist as soon as possible. The possible subsequent investigation of the site will call upon a whole range of interesting underwater skills in which you and your diving companions may become most interested and expert. If a wreck is of archaeological importance it may be registered under the Protection of Wrecks Act 1973. This act restricts legal access to a named group of persons. The Protection of Military Remains Act 1986 may also apply.

However most of the wrecks visited by divers are of modern date and if you merely wish to dive on them, and examine them photographically or otherwise you have none of the problems outlined above. However wreck diving presents a large range of special hazards of which you must be aware. Wrecks are, in the main, corroded hulks of jagged, rusting, weakened and twisted metal. Weakened structures may collapse without warning and bury or cut the diver. You may get trapped or lost within the wreck if you have disturbed

silt inside. You may be bitten by a conger eel, a typical denizen of a wreck. You may hit your head on an overhead structure or get caught in a net lost on the wreck by an unfortunate fisherman. Some wrecks will contain unexploded shells or even dangerous chemicals to add to your hazards.

If you plan to enter a wreck it is a good idea to take two precautions in your planning at a very early stage. 1. Try and ascertain the general state of corrosion and damage to the wreck. A wreck which sank with little immediate damage to the hull and superstructures a few years ago will probably be in a fairly safe state though you might of course easily get lost within it. 2. Obtain an exact plan of the boat from the builders or at least a typical plan of that type of boat from standard books on modern ships.

Transfer parts of the plan to underwater slates so that you can refer to the plan underwater. Note that damaged wrecks may seem at first sight to bear no relation at all to anything you have on your plan and it may take a lot of careful inspection before you begin to understand which part of a wreck is which. If the wreck is of steel and has been underwater for forty years or more, it is likely to be approaching the point at which many structures are seriously weakened by corrosion so great care will be called for if you enter it.

We list below some of the simple rules for safe wreck diving.

1. Drop anchor up current of the wreck, allow your boat to drift back and use a shotline to the wreck. This precaution prevents you damaging the wreck by dropping your anchor on it. It also prevents the likely event that your anchor will snag on the wreck.

2. Be especially careful to ensure that you have more than enough air for the dive since it may take you much longer to get out of the wreck than you anticipated.

3. Make sure that your own equipment is so arranged that it has no features that might snag on the wreck. Long second stage hoses run under rather than over your shoulder and inverted air cylinders may help to avoid snagging.

4. Do not enter a wreck unless (a) hatches or other sites of entry are secured open (b) you have a fairly good idea of the probable internal layout (c) you are carrying a working torch and (d) a light non-buoyant line you can lay out as you work inwards so that you can retrace your route out of the wreck along the line.

5. Do not enter a wreck merely because your buddy wants to do so.

6. Be very careful about where you put your hands or feet.

7. Look in all directions before making a move.

8. Do not touch anything you are unable to identify.

9. Do not take out your demand valve and breathe from what appears to be an air pocket. These gas pockets may contain lethal concentrations of carbon dioxide, hydrogen sulphide or other gases.

10. Do not remove objects from the wreck unless you have permission or unless they are essential for identification of a previously unknown and unidentified wreck.

Legal aspects

The Law on wreck diving and salvage is specific and principally contained in *Part 9 Merchant Shipping Act 1984, The Civil Aviation Act 1949,* and *The Protection of Wrecks Act 1973.* The legal language is as clear as it usually is to the layman, but these Acts basically state that any object found on the seabed, either on or in the vicinity of any wreck or wreckage which is removed by the finder with the intention of keeping it is an act of theft. The maximum punishment is fourteen years imprisonment. You would also be guilty of an offence even if the object you removed from the seabed didn't seem to have anything to do with the wreck. If the owner of a wreck has given you permission to remove articles from a wreck, then you would not be breaking the law. So, any object found outside UK territorial waters and brought to the UK or any objects of wreckage found inside UK waters and brought ashore must in all cases be handed to the local Receiver of Wrecks who will be able to tell you what rights you have to the objects.

As mentioned earlier, marine law is specific and very comprehensive, however if it is safe to dive, then you can dive on most wrecks around the UK, with the exception of certain military wrecks and wrecks protected under the 1973 Act. Exploring wrecks adds a new dimension to diving and produces all kinds of emotions from the excitement of seeing sunlight streak down across a section of superstructure covered in orange soft corals to the uncertainty of peering inside a gloomy boiler-house door hoping to avoid the lurking eels.

Salvage

This is a specialist subject which requires experience, great tenacity of character, great resource and a good deal of luck. However the simpler types of salvage, for instance of boats up to a few tons size or of objects of up to a few hundred pounds weight underwater are well within the capabilities of small groups of amateur divers. The bibliography in the appendix to the Manual contains a section on simpler salvage methods and if your interest lies in this direction we suggest you consult these books, or follow the advice set out below.

Raising a small yacht is an exploit that should be well within the capabilities of a small group of amateur divers, yet it is carried out so infrequently that advice may be useful.

Let's assume that the yacht is undamaged or only very slightly damaged, so that it is both feasible and desirable to raise it and float it on the surface. The salvage divides itself into the following stages.

1. Reconnaissance.
2. Removal of loose and light gear, including if possible part of the ballast (if present).
3. Preparations for lifting (including minor repair).
4. The lift.
5. Obtaining enough freeboard to be able to bail out the boat.

Reconnaissance and preliminaries

If you are lucky enough to be given a true position for the boat, reconnaissance is no more than assessing the depth and attitude at which she is lying, the extent of the damage, the nature of the bottom and any special problems that might occur during a lift. If the boat is not buoyed already, buoy her. During reconnaissance you might start removing all light gear and anything that is floatable if a boat is available overhead to pick up floating gear. Working on a 2½ ton sail yacht with auxiliary and cabin we used the first dive to clear the cabin of clothing, bedding and to close the portholes and ventilators. If the cabin is dark or the water muddy have one diver work in the cabin and the other stay just outside – if the cabin is small this will be necessary in all conditions.

Removal of the ballast lightens the load you are going to have to lift, but it means that the boat is much less stable once you lift her. You want to avoid a capsize on the surface at all costs so there is a strong argument for leaving quite a lot of ballast in, particularly if the mast of the yacht cannot easily be removed underwater. The problem with a mast is that once you begin to raise the boat the mast will be the first object to protrude above the surface and unless you have a low centre of gravity in the boat, and a good deal of weight low down, the mast may easily pull the boat over.

The ballast can easily be put into a pail and lifted to the surface piece by piece by a boatman.

Preparations for the lift

A. Sealing small leaks. Adequate sealing of small holes up to ¼ inch wide can be made with plasticine hammered into place. Holes up to 2″ diameter can be adequately plugged with cloth around a piece of wood. Holes up to 6″ in each direction can be partially plugged with plastic sheet and plyboard but a watertight job is impossible and you and the boat owner will have to be content with a raising of the boat to the surface and a tow to a tidal shore at high water or to a slip. Larger holes are probably beyond the resources of an amateur diver though if they are above the normal waterline of the boat they will not affect refloating.

Don't forget that a boat may have portholes, ventilators, hawse pipes, sea cocks, as normal fittings which water can get through. Close or seal these off before raising.

B. Buoyancy containers and Lifting Bags, etc.

The principles of lifting are to:

1. Attach your flotation devices securely to the boat at the lowest possible position you can. If the floats are above deck level you will end up with the deck a few feet under the surface and with the floats possibly in a very dangerous position. If a float is full of air on the surface it will probably spill air out of itself and fill with water and you will have compounded the original disaster. If the floats are low down the boat will reach the surface and, with sufficient lift, lie with much of its upperwork above water with the lifting devices still underwater where they exert maximum lift and cannot be capsized.

2. Bring the boat up on an even keel. If the boat is lying unevenly it will be worthwhile using partial lift to get her onto an even keel and this may assist fitting the lifting bridles.

3. Ensure that you have reserve flotation devices fitted which can be filled with air so that any leakage from or damage to a flotation device does not cause a second sinking. Fill these with air on reaching the surface.

4. Calculation of the amount of air required for lifting can be done if you know what the specific gravity and dead weight of the boat are. But you probably cannot get such information. The first simple formula below gives good results if you know these things. Otherwise discover the approximate weight of keel (if any) and remaining ballast and of any engine that is fitted. Assume that these items are made of iron, of specific gravity 7.9 and use the second formula.

Formula 1. To calculate volume of air required to lift an object (e.g. boat).

$$\text{Weight of boat out of water in kg.} \quad - \quad \frac{\text{Weight of boat out of water in kg.}}{\text{Specific gravity}}$$

gives litres of air at ambient pressure required to lift this boat in fresh water.

Formula 2.

$$\text{Weight of iron or steel parts out of water in kg.} \quad - \quad \frac{\text{Weight of iron or steel parts out of water in kg.}}{7.9}$$

gives number of litres of air required at ambient pressure.

If the boat is made of wood and is recently sunk you may get appreciable buoyancy from this – fibreglass will however give no buoyancy. Having estimated the volume of the lift required acquire about four times as much lifting power. The reason for this is not because your figures are wrong, though they may be, but because errors plus the need to raise quite a lot of the boat above the water mean that much more lifting power is needed.

Flotation devices may be lifting bags, lifting boxes made from chemical carboys, oil drums or chemical bottles. In many ways the 10 gallon chemical bottles with handles, that agricultural sprays etc, are delivered in, form the best lifting device. 10 gallons of air lifts 100lbs weight in water and only represents just over 1½ cubic feet of air at surface pressure. 40 gallon oil drums are good but unwieldy and as supplied have entry holes that are far too small for safety. Obviously your lifting device must have a free gap for excess air to escape through as it expands on the way to the surface. You have two choices about lifting devices. If they are full of air at the bottom then as they lift upwards they do not become any more buoyant. If your lifting devices are only partially filled with air at the bottom it expands as your boat surfaces and the buoyancy bags become still more buoyant. This may turn a controlled lift into a disastrous race to the surface which may terminate in the boat capsizing. So most of the buoyancy devices should be completely filled with air. Another problem comes from the fact that if air expands inside a partially filled container water must be driven out. Water is rather viscous stuff and may not leave the container sufficiently rapidly unless you have large holes in it; if this delay happens you may burst your container, followed by a rapid sinking. So 40 gallon oil drums may need a couple of 6″ diameter holes in their bases to allow water to be driven out by expanded air. Obviously if your buoyancy containers are full of air and open to the water on their undersurface, there will be no need to force water out of them so that there is much less risk of bursting them.

So you are faced with the requirements that you have as much of your buoyancy in containers which are completely filled with air and which will be underwater when the boat surfaces. You also need to ensure that the lift is arranged so that the boat comes up level. How do you achieve all this?

Since any calculation that you may make about the buoyancy lift required is so likely to be wrong it is a good idea to work with small buoyancy units, i.e. adding 10 gallon containers one by one is likely to give you much more control than if you have just two eighty gallon containers and start filling them with air. Another rule is to ensure stability by placing the main lift under the heaviest parts of the boat and to have containers on either side of the beamiest parts of the boat. Thus if you were to put the lift at bow and stern alone you would have almost no control of the lateral stability of the boat, while a lift balanced on either side of the beamiest part of the boat would give you good lateral control but might allow the boat to come up bow or stern down. So the best solution seems to be put the lift in four places. One pair of sets of containers on either side of the hull at mast level and the other set on either side of the hull at engine level will give you maximum stability. Amongst other things this arrangement will give you virtual certainty that the centre of gravity of the boat lies between your four sets of lifting containers – this is essential for a controlled lift. A possible arrangement is shown below.

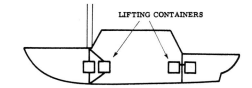

Fig. 87.

When attaching the containers do not tie them onto the deck fittings. First of all, deck fittings are not necessarily all that strong and second, the containers will be too high being above deck level. The lifting containers have to be positioned well down the sides of the hull and the method of achieving this is to construct some form of bridle around the boat running under the keel. One way of fixing these bridles is illustrated below. Obviously your rope work must be impeccable because if anything breaks, slips or unties during the lift, you will be in trouble. Strains of 400 lbs are quite easily set up even lifting a small boat. It is also desirable to use rope that does not stretch under strain. Suggestions are that you use hemp of at least 1 inch circumference. Knots must be strong and at any point where lines are attached to the bridles you must use knots that

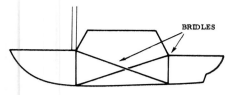

Fig. 88.

form a bight in the bridle – otherwise the lines may slip upwards on the bridles once tension is applied. If that happens you will end up with the containers floating above the mid-line of the boat. If you have the time to fix carabineer clips onto the lifting lines, you may find rigging the lifting devices quicker.

It is a good idea to slip the lines under the hull when forming the bridles by lifting first the bow and then the stern a few feet by containers tied to bow or stern. This makes it easy to rig the bridles and also gives you some idea about how much lift may be needed totally. Don't forget to deflate these containers and allow the boat to settle back onto an even keel before the lift.

Make sure before you lift that any boom is secured in midline or removed – otherwise if it starts swinging a capsize and a diving accident are very likely.

The lift

Choose a calm day for the lift – the consequence of doing anything else are all too clear.

Attach a line from the boat to a mooring buoy or attendant boat so that you don't lose her sideways after the lift.

The important feature of diving operations during the lifting process is that as few divers as possible should be around underwater. Ideally one diver should fill the containers and one diver should accompany him for safety reasons. The containers should be filled in such a sequence that first one container at one lifting point is filled, then the opposite one, then one at the other lifting bridles and then fourth the container opposite it. Watch the boat for signs of lifting. If it begins to move fin out of the way. If there is no movement, fill a second set of containers in the sequence described and so on. At some point she'll start to lift and if this is bow or stern upwards add more air to the set of containers at the opposite end of the boat. With a little skill you should be able to get a nice controlled lift on an even keel.

At the surface fill all containers that had not been filled already. So long as you keep the boat on an even keel, this gives you extra stability and protects you against the effects of leakage of air from any of the lifting containers.

After the lift

At this point you'll probably have the boat with its upperworks partly out of the water but you are unlikely to have freeboard all the way round. If the cockpit bulwarks are still underwater you'll have to add extra lift under the stern but this should be easy to arrange now you are working in only a few feet depth of water. Reducing the lift in the forward set of containers may also help by throwing the stern upwards. Removal of more of the ballast will now be feasible and unlikely to damage the stability of the boat and will tend to give you more freeboard. Underwater the wooden or fibreglass parts of the boat had almost no weight (or maybe some buoyancy) but once above water they may weigh hundreds of pounds. The 2½ ton yacht we raised took about 600 lbs of lift to bring to the surface but another 2,400 lbs of lift to get a freeboard of one inch around the cockpit. By this time the cabin was mostly above water.

Finally, one diver got into the boat and, taking care not to destabilise the boat, by getting in over the stern and crouching down, was able to start bailing. In about ten minutes enough bailing had been done to give six inches freeboard and then it was time to invite the non-divers to come and help bailing. If you had access to a suitable hand pump or electric pump you might be able to make much lighter of this part of the work because in the instance of the 2½ ton yacht approximately one ton of water had to be bailed out by hand.

B NIGHT DIVING

Many divers find night diving more satisfying than any other type of diving. This might seem surprising to any one who has little knowledge and who has never tried it. There are several particular attractions to night diving. Chief amongst these is the brightness of the colours of the underwater world when seen by torch underwater at night. Then there is the fact that many animals emerge from their hiding places only at night, while you can usually approach close to fish which lie almost mesmerised in the light of a torch. You may also have the pleasure of experiencing an underwater display of phosphorescence which can be so bright that you need no torch. The reason incidentally why colours appear brighter at night is that you see them by your torchlight which is rich in red while during the daytime you see by blue-green light and this tends to dominate the illumination even when you use a torch.

However there are problems with night diving. You should be aware of the problems and the solutions before you dive.

1. Entering and leaving the water is difficult when you cannot see clearly. Thus falls and slips are likely.

2. Finding your way about underwater at night can be difficult. It is clearly very inconvenient if you surface at night far away from your point of entry, whether boat or shore. Surface cover whether from boat or by a snorkeller is nearly impossible. In the remote event of an accident, whether above or underwater, rescue is going to be more difficult than in daytime.

The solutions to these problems are basically ones which ensure that you as a diver can see your surroundings and ones which ensure that you can see both under and above water. But in addition there are various special precautions to be taken because vision and visibility are poor at the best of times even with the best equipped divers.

The following items of additional equipment are needed:

1. At least one torch per diver. Torches must be attached to your harness by a lanyard and quick release clip so that you will not lose the torch if you let it fall from your hand. Head mounted torches, usually on a rigid helmet have the great advantage that both your hands are free for other purposes. This is particularly advantageous if you are photographing by night when both hands are likely to be needed to operate the camera. Most torches have a light-time of between thirty and sixty minutes. Bear in mind that you will probably use your torch while kitting up and while getting into the water so that the effective light-time underwater may be quite short. There is much to be said for rechargable torches for although they have a high initial cost the running expense is low, unlike the situation with torches that need new batteries after each night dive. Make sure that your torch has a new battery or is fully charged before setting out for a night

dive and make sure before you enter the water that all closures on the torch are tightly closed.

2. Fluorescent overhoods for each diver to wear on their heads. These 'dayglo' hoods make it easy for divers to spot each other underwater and for shore or boat parties to observe divers on the surface. They are not essential items but greatly ease night diving.

3. Electronic 'flashers' or repetitive strobes which emit a very bright flash every one or two seconds are very useful, though not essential, items of equipment for night diving. Since these can be seen for miles on the surface even in bad weather and for scores of metres underwater even in poor visibility they are excellent devices to enable two divers to find each other should they lose contact and for surface parties to track divers both underwater and on the surface. Ideally they should be mounted on your back at about neck height so that they can be seen from above with ease. If the diver holds such a flasher underneath him it cannot be seen easily from the surface.

4. A shore or boat based light to mark the exit point for divers. This should not be very bright but should be distinctive in colour or flash so that divers can recognise it easily.

When you are using a torch in night diving remember to avoid shining it into the face of a nearby diver. If you do commit this crime he or she will be dazzled. If you are making a hand signal to your fellow diver point the beam obliquely so that it does not fall on his face and make the hand signal in the beam in a position where he or she can see it. You can use your torch as an additional signalling aid, see Fig. 89. If you lose each other turn round, pointing your torch outwards so that your companion will have a good chance of spotting you, and you of him while he rotates his torch. It is often much easier to find your companion by night than by day if you both have torches and use them in this way.

Obviously if two groups of divers are close to each other and one becomes separated from his or her companion he or she may easily try and join the wrong group. For this reason dive groups should be kept apart and large numbers of divers should not be on a night dive.

If your torch or your companion's torch starts to fade or is suddenly extinguished make your way as a group towards the surface. It is not wholly safe for two divers to rely upon one torch.

Night dives are conducted in much the same way as daytime dives but the Dive Leader and

Fig. 89. Signals for night diving. (a) 'OK all is well' (question or answer as appropriate), large slow circles with the lamp. (b) Alternative OK signal if the divers are close together, note that the signal is the same as in daytime. (c) 'Something wrong' (question or answer), large rapid to and fro motions with the lamp, arm extended.

his/her companion for each dive must take care – particular care:

1. To check that they know the visual marks and lights marking the boat or place or shore entry.

2. To have rehearsed lamp signals that may be used between divers or between divers and shore.

3. To have arranged that everyone diving knows what to do should they become separated from their companion underwater.

4. To have arranged procedures in the event of separation, see above.

If you surface because you failed to find your companion within two minutes do not attempt to search underwater again unless you can see the light marking them clearly from the surface. If there is possibility of confusion with the lights of another dive group do not dive. If you surface separated from your companion it is likely that he or she will make their way back on the surface to the point of entry though it is of course desirable for you to use your torches to find each other and to exchange 'OK' signals on the surface.

Obviously night dive sites should be chosen with care. They should have easy entry if they are shore sites and should ideally be known already to all divers. Sites with currents should be avoided. Obviously night diving in appreciable waves or swell is hazardous. If you use a boat appreciate that boatmen will be more apprehensive about approaching a shore at night than in the day. Again, if you use a boat for night diving ensure that it is anchored before any diver enters the water, and that it remains anchored until all divers have sur-

faced and got aboard. It is exceedingly hard to be sure that you can spot all divers on the surface before you've collided with them with your boat underway.

Bear in mind that all equipment should be especially well secured. Equipment lost at night is rarely found again. Also remember that night-time air temperatures are usually lower than those in the daytime. Consequently divers may easily get chilled on night-time dives. Watch for signs of this and have plenty of hot drinks available on boat or shore.

C DIVING IN CURRENTS

Diving in currents which are running at speeds greater than half a knot presents problems to the diver. A fairly fit diver can make headway against a current of up to 1½ knots for quite long periods, but his or her air consumption will rise and progress will be quite slow near the upper limit of this range of current speed. Thus a dive in such currents when you have to put a lot of extra exertion and time into overcoming the current is a dive in which you waste time and air. The solutions to such problems are:

1. Dive at another time when the current is less appreciable or absent, see Ch. 10 for methods of estimating such times.

2. Plan the place and method of diving so that you minimise the effect of current on your dive, or even take advantage of it to improve your dive plan. This section of the manual deals with such solutions.

If the current runs against the diver even more strongly progress against the current becomes more and more difficult even for short periods and at 2 knots generally impossible. Even staying in one position by finning will be tiring and difficult. Above 2½ knots even holding yourself in position on a line or solid object on the bottom will be very difficult and as the current increases the risk of having your mask or demand valve or other equipment pulled out of place or off you by the current becomes an appreciable one. Obviously you must be aware of procedures to follow if you find yourself unexpectedly being overcome by a current, and thus this section also covers:

3. Emergency procedures if caught in too strong a current.

There are four aspects to current diving:

A. Minimising the effects of currents.

B. Procedures to adopt if you meet unexpected currents.

C. Procedures for staying in place in a current.

D. Drift diving with the current, when you allow the current to move you over a long distance.

Always remember that though we have written just above of currents as lateral movement of water, and although this is the most usual meaning of the word, descending or ascending currents may occur in certain places at certain times and of these descending currents are by far the most dangerous for a diver.

The majority of currents are generated tidally and represent the flow of water to meet the tidal rise or away from the tidal fall in an area. When tides rising and falling at different times meet, say at a headland you may get very strong currents. For instance the tide rises earlier in the Sound of Jura than on the west side of Jura so that the flood tide tends to run out through the Corryvreckan, while the ebb current starts flowing out of the Sound of Jura southwestwards while the tide is still rising at the North end of the Sound of Jura because of the influx of water through the Corryvreckan. In this area slack water tends to be in mid tide. Currents may also be wind generated. For example if a heavy sea breaks against a steep cliff water will be piled against the cliff and this may lead to a descending current running down the cliff-face or slope underwater and a seaward bottom current in front of the cliff. A wind behind a current on the surface will generally accelerate the surface current. Abnormally high or low barometric pressure, particularly when prolonged at a particular site may generate or modify local currents. Heavy rainfall or snow-melt on nearby land may alter currents in estuaries and sea-lochs.

Minimising the effects of currents

Before diving obtain all the information you can from the appropriate pilot book, local chart or other source and use these together with the tide tables to predict the time, strength and direction of any current. Bear in mind that local topography and weather conditions may modify the time and strength of the current. Once you've done this in the pre-planning stage of a dive you will usually be able to choose a slack-water or near slack-water time. Usually you should plan to start your dive slightly before the start of the slack so that an early slack or delay on the way to the site will not lead to your missing a dive. It is also a comfort to divers if they know that any current they meet is likely to diminish during the course of the dive.

When diving bear in mind that a slight current may help you by clearing away any sediment that you may stir up so long as you move up current. Letting yourself drift down current may be easy diving but it is apt to ensure that you stay in the water you've muddied by your own finning if you are one of those divers who is an incautious finner or mud-puppy or if you had to work on the bottom. Moreover if you drift down current you may well have to exert yourself to get back to the entry point at a time in the dive when you are tiring. If you move up current slowly in the first half of the dive you'll stay in clean water and your return to the entry point should be easy.

Despite the rude remarks we made about 'mud-puppy' divers you will find, in stronger currents, that keeping close to the bottom will keep you out of the full strength of the bottom. If the current is very strong you may find it necessary to pull yourself along the bottom holding onto rocks etc, but if there is nothing to grasp you are simply going to have to let go, see later for ensuing procedure.

Finning with even a weak current will greatly accelerate your rate of movement so that you may easily be unaware of the distance you have covered. Conversely finning up current will be slowed and you may be surprised how long it takes to cover even a modest distance. Finning across a current will alter your path even if you are following a good compass bearing because although your orientation may be correct the current is moving you laterally all the time. It is very difficult for a diver to make allowance for this. If visibility is good and the bottom has clear marks on it like prominent rocks it may be possible to sight a correct compass course from one landmark to the next and to follow this. But in the absence of such good conditions following compass courses across currents becomes a most inaccurate method of finding your way about.

Procedures in unexpected currents

If you find yourself diving in a current which you did not expect bear in mind that it may increase your air consumption or lead you to misjudge your position. Your very first reaction should be to turn into the current, note its direction on your compass and discover whether you can fin against it effectively. If you can make progress against it which can only be judged if you can see a reference point such as the seabed your next stop should be to decide whether the current is going to alter your dive plan. If your plan was, for example, to fin about 200m in a direction which turns out to be upcurrent, you should quickly make a judgement as to whether you will be able to carry out all or an appreciable part of the plan with the time and air you have available. You may decide that the original plan has little or no chance of working. If so surface and discuss a new plan, perhaps hanging onto the side of an inflatable or to a buoy. If you carry a slate to explain your change in plans in full you may be able to do this underwater. Remember, as we said in Ch. 6 that it can be hazardous to change a dive plan underwater, particularly without discussion because your fellow diver must be quite clear as to your intentions – in addition your surface cover or dive marshal usually needs to know your plans. Don't forget that the current may be increasing or changing direction somewhat during the planned course of your dive.

If it is clear immediately that the current is going to sweep you away fin diagonally across the curent and in the general direction of the shore point of entry if you can or towards the boat. Surfacing fairly rapidly is usually the best policy as you can see your objective and be seen but bear in mind that currents usually run most rapidly at the surface. On occasion it may be possible to pull yourself along the bottom by holding onto rocks and large stones. If you already know the site you may know that this

method will bring you to the shore or alternatively take you only a short distance when you might find your progress stopped by a sandy bottom with nothing on it to grip.

If you are caught in a descending current or suspect that you might be, watch your depth gauge carefully, so that you check your rate of descent and rapidly discover whether you can fin against it. If you cannot make headway, inflate your ABLJ and if this fails drop your weight belt. Descending currents are most dangerous on cliffs and steep descents but this type of bottom offers the advantage that you can climb it hand over hand if other methods of ascent fail or work poorly.

Once you have surfaced it will be a great comfort if you can signal up your cover boat and be taken aboard before you have drifted far. Obviously your companion diver should stay as close as possible to you both underwater and on the surface, while awaiting pickup. If however the cover boat fails to spot you due to high waves, inadvertance, break-down or poor visibility (as in fog) bear in mind that you can stay afloat and reasonably warm in a wet suit in British waters for 24 to 48 hours. During this time you are very likely to be drifted ashore or very close to shore. Nevertheless it would be wise to carry personal diver's flares so that you can make an emergency signal. If you failed to have a cover boat you should be alright but you have placed yourself at greater risk by diving in a current without surface cover.

Procedures for staying in one place in a current

If you are diving on one fixed spot or in a small area in a site which is apt to be swept by currents you need a series of procedures to ensure that you can do this.

One simple rule is to dive only at slack or in slackening water. A second rule is to rig a shot line with a suitable distance line on the bottom to take you to all parts of the site that you might wish to visit. If you feel that you must attach yourself to the shot line during a dive use a short line with a quick-release clip at either end. Fix one end to a loop round the shot and the other quick-release to your harness in an easily accessible place. Your companion diver could be attached to you by a short buddy line with similar quick-releases at either end. The advantage of using these short lines is that you do not have to spend all your time attending to the line and you have two hands available for other purposes should you need them. The disadvantage is that your progress may be impeded if the line(s) snag. If the current is flowing appreciably the shot will lie at an angle to the vertical and you should ensure that the current does not press you against the shot so take care during descent or ascent.

The shot-weight should be appreciable. 20 kilograms might be a minimum value. The flotation (buoyancy) in the top float plus the possible buoyancy of the divers plus the component of lift in the shot as the current tends to pull it out at an angle must not exceed the bottom weight. If it does your shot will drift away. Remember that even if your shot line is no longer than the depth of water the current will tend to pull it out until the line is taut to the bottom. In this situation insufficient bottom weight will cause the shot to come off the bottom, while if there is sufficient bottom weight any additional weight on the line, as from divers descending may pull the float under. Consequently it is a good idea to have a light line and small float attached to the top of the shot to mark its position on the surface. A shot-weight of 25 kilograms might be appropriately matched by a buoy of 15 kilograms buoyancy allowing 10 kilograms of diver's weight and current drag on the line.

If the current becomes so strong during a dive that you find your mask or demand valve being clawed at by the flow of water try to face directly into or directly down current so that the current cannot pull this equipment to one side. Abandon the dive and ascend the shot if possible. If you find that it is impossible to stay on the shot make sure that any companion divers with you know that and agree that you are all going to leave the shot. If you all let go the shot simultaneously the force of current will immediately drop off as you move with the current. Then ascend as rapidly as consonant with safety. But note that this procedure is an emergency one and a deviation from dive plan which will not be expected by the surface cover, though they should be aware in general terms of such a possibility in such a site.

Obviously such diving requires careful consideration. You must use a safety boat and it should ideally be standing off a little down current from the shot. If the boat ties to the top of the shot it must be able to leave the shot, start its engine and get underway rapidly in the event of anyone surfacing off the shot. If a large boat is being used for diving it is a very good idea to have a heavy rigged floating line

ready on deck which can be trailed by the boat across the path of any surface divers so that they can all be brought on board quickly and safely.

Drift diving

The alternative to staying in one place is to use the current to take you from one place to another. Procedures are entirely different from those needed when you intend to stay in one place. Drift diving enables you to cover great distances rapidly though you usually cannot stop or go back upcurrent to look twice at an interesting piece of site.

Drift diving requires a lot of preplanning. First you must make a good assessment of the current strength and direction during your planned dive. Study a chart carefully unless you know the site exceedingly well, so that you can plot out a drift dive which will remain near the bottom at a constant or nearly constant depth. The reason for this is that this type of diving requires the use of a marker float on each diver (or at least each group of divers). If the depth is changing rapidly as you are swept across the site you will be spending most of your time altering the length of line on the surface or float marker. Decide your entry point and probable exit (surfacing) positions at this stage. If you decide that your proposed drift dive might take you into overfalls change the dive site because the underwater turbulence will dismay, disrupt and perhaps even endanger the divers and the surface turbulence will dismay any boatman.

Equipment. Surface markers or floats.

Each dive group must carry either one surface marker per diver or a surface marker plus a buddy line.

Each diver must have a compass as well as all usual diving equipment.

Surface, float or 'blob' markers are essential for this type of diving. The use of such markers has given rise to much heated argument amongst divers, some maintaining that they are an invaluable safety aid on all dives, whilst others regard them as anathema. We point out that they always give the surface cover a definite indication as to the position of the divers. Furthermore the surface cover can use the marker to make a rope signal to the divers if he is worried about their state or wishes them to surface. In the event of non-response or over-stay at depth the standby diver has an infallible means of finding the divers. The only disadvantages are that the line from diver to the float may become entangled in such things as heavy kelp, other buoys and their lines and that in some conditions i.e. appreciable surface wind, appreciable depth of current, the line and marker may drag so much on the diver that progress becomes impossibly slow.

Our advice is that the following types of dive require surface float markers on each dive group or diver.

A. Drift dives.

B. Dives in which it is intended to explore a large or fairly large area at moderate or shallow depth. (Exploring large areas at considerable depth is in itself an unwise diving procedure).

C. Diving in areas with extensive presence or possible presence of surface craft.

On the other hand some types of dive are unsuitable for surface markers. These include:

A. Diving on shot lines.

B. Diving under heavy kelp or amongst a dense collection of moorings, both of which are likely to snag the lines from the divers to the markers.

C. Diving amongst overhanging and irregular rocks.

D. Deep diving, particularly if currents are present. In such types of diving shot lines are advised, see Ch. 8.

If you are making some other type of dive we consider it advisable to use a surface marker on each group of divers but appreciate that inexperience or the nature of the dive may incline you to different solutions.

There is one large problem with surface markers; namely no ideal design has yet been produced.

Three designs are shown in Fig. 57. The simplest is the H frame and small surface buoy. The diver winds light line, say 0.5 cm diameter braided nylon, onto or off his or her H frame so that the line is taut to a small floating marker on the surface. The trouble with this type is that the diver must spend a lot of time winding out or winding in the buoy. If the buoy and line float are slack on the surface the diver is poorly marked, the line may easily snag on other objects or even on itself and a lot of slack has to be taken up if the surface cover is to signal to the diver. The RN uses the blob float. Here the line unwinds spontaneously from the float as the diver descends. The

length of line on the float corresponds to the maximum depth of the dive. As the diver ascends the line tends to float slack as he has no easy way of winding it taut. This type of blob may unwind spontaneously in certain sea conditions. The third type is a reel of line and float. The diver carries the reel which unwinds spontaneously on descent. Unnecessary unwinding can be stopped with a pawl. When the diver ascends he winds the line onto the reel.

The surface marker should, from the point of view of visibility be as large as possible, but such a design would make it very susceptible to wind action. Wind effects would be minimised by a very small float. The ideal design would be a reel which would act automatically as the diver ascends or descends and whose float would be unaffected by wind or current, while retaining high surface visibility. Many of these requirements are mutually incompatible.

Procedures

Having planned your drift dive, equipped yourself appropriately and become familiar with surface marker floats you are ready for drift diving.

Descent at the start of the dive should be rapid so that you do not lose your sense of position. If the visibility is low you will find your drift dive probably rather unrewarding though there is for some a certain excitement in being rushed up to rocks that appear suddenly out of the gloom. If the current is at all strong use a buddy-line. The reason for this is that you may otherwise find that the current drifts two divers apart as they progress with it. The divers should check their general direction of movement by taking bearings on approaching objects. They should also check depth frequently. If the direction of movement or the depth differ appreciably from your plan abandon your dive because you have clearly made some miscalculation. Abandon the dive if you find yourselves in appreciable turbulence.

The greatest hazard of this type of dive lies in getting swept into nets. Obviously it is possible to take account of fixed nets such as salmon bag nets in planning the dive and in any event such nets are usually very shallow. The real risk lies in getting swept into abandoned or snagged nets lying on the bottom. To minimise such risks surface while you still have 50 bar or more air just in case you were to be swept into a net at the end of your dive. Look ahead and up throughout the dive. Carry a very sharp knife, attached by a line or cord to your scabbard or harness so that you cannot lose it. It is possible to cut yourself or another diver out of a net in two to three minutes even if badly snagged in a strong new net provided you have a sharp knife.

Remember that you must have a cover boat with an experienced and fully briefed boatman. There is one possible exception to this requirement. If diving in narrow shallow channels it may be permissible to rely on a quick retreat to shore at the end of the dive. Do not carry out drift dives in fairways or in situations which might sweep you into fairways.

Above all remember that you should never plan a drift dive as one in which decompression will be required. You should take great care to avoid even a slight chance that decompression will have to be done for if you do have to carry out a stop you will be drifting around in the water trying to carry out a stop in a situation for which you are quite unlikely to be too buoyant.

Chapter 9

Branch Instructor Qualification

INTRODUCTION

The Scottish Sub-Aqua Club is the National Governing Body for the sport in Scotland and has built up an enviable reputation over the years for its safety record and high training standards.

This part of the manual is the result of over thirty seven years of diver training with the content being refined by very experienced diver teachers, many of them professionally qualified in the world of education.

It takes years of training to become a professional teacher so it would be naive to imagine that a few days (or weeks) on a diver instructor's course will produce the perfect instructor. Diving is essentially a practical pastime and the same is true in diver instruction. Much practise will be required after the initial course with the instructor constantly reviewing the effectiveness of his/her methods. The purpose of this section is to provide a source of material to enable organisers to run standardised courses and to act as a reference guide for practising dive instructors.

The chapter starts with the contents of the lectures in the Training Course for Branch Instructors.

LECTURES

LECTURE 1

Aims and Objectives of the Course (20-30 min)

1.1 *Course administration and organisation*

The presenter should introduce themself, even if it appears unnecessary. There may be a few candidates present who do not know the presenter and an initial introduction helps set the scene and mood of the course. The presenter's qualifications and credentials should be mentioned to help establish authority.

The main objective should then be stated initially, that is that this course is to introduce and train divers to instruct to the Scottish Sub-Aqua Club Branch Instructor standard. The point should be made that the course constitutes part of the process of becoming an instructor and the candidates will not be qualified or even formally assessed during the course.

The course staff should then be introduced or described, followed by a brief description of the course sequence. The lecture rooms, pool and any other venues should be described with location details and timings. Equipment required by candidates should also be described. The cost should be mentioned with the timing of the collection of the fees. This should ideally be at this first meeting.

The candidates should be identified, possibly by name tags, perhaps with each one being given the chance to introduce themselves. The Course organiser should take a written note of all those attending and check their log books for current medicals, 3rd class diver award and current SSAC membership. Non-SSAC divers are welcome to attend but normally instructor courses are not directly cross-certifiable unless some agreed prior arrangements have been concluded between the Clubs concerned.

1.2 *Aims and objectives*

The aim shall be to train and ensure that successful candidates are properly qualified to instruct small groups of would-be divers in all aspects of diving up to 2nd class open water work or their own diver grade if higher. The Branch Instructor (formally Instructor I), is active primarily at branch level and is competent to teach diving theory and skills in a lecture room, swimming pool and open water. During the course, appropriate teaching methods and techniques will be described.

1.3 *Safety*

This should be emphasised during each stage of the course with guidelines being provided as appropriate. In particular, fire routines, assembly points, pool evacuation signals and the use of safety officers.

LECTURE 2

The Role and Qualities to be expected from a Branch Instructor (40-60 min)

2.1 *Qualities*
This will be described first since the implementation of these qualities partly forms the role of the instructor.

A new member who is taught by a good instructor will learn good habits from the very beginning. Conversely, a new member taught by a bad instructor will pick up bad practices which will be very difficult to remedy later. Therefore it is of great importance that SSAC instructors teach to a uniform, high standard.

A dive instructor is more than just a teacher. A self instructional text could be regarded as a 'teacher'. The Instructor has to convey a sense of wonder and excitement to the trainee, in a strange, potentially hostile environment while still maintaining a responsible and safe attitude.

The qualities that make a good instructor are to some extent inborn but with some application and enthusiasm, the necessary qualities can be acquired and developed within most divers.

2.1.1 *Authority*
Instructor needs to gain confidence and respect of the trainees. (a) Instructor must be clearly identifiable to the trainee. (b) Instructor needs an air of confidence. (c) Confidence should be based on knowledge, experience and modesty, not on an overpowering or boastful attitude. (d) Instructor should be friendly and approachable. (e) Instructor needs to keep control by a firm but friendly discipline. (f) Instructor must always be discreet and consistent.

2.1.2 *Communications*
It is important to use the best and most appropriate methods. In the case of language for example, use words and phrases that would be comprehensible to the candidates. Good communications means the instructor being able to understand the trainee's point of view and adjusting their presentation of material to suit the trainee(s).

2.1.3 *Professionalism*
The instructor should be beyond reasonable criticism in his behaviour towards his group of trainees. This means punctuality, good preparation of material, suitable appearance (being not under- or over-dressed).

2.1.4 *Patience*
A necessary virtue with slower learners. In the teaching situation, if success is slow or apparently non-existant, then this should be regarded as the instructor's fault, not the trainee's fault. If one teaching approach does not work, then an alternative approach should be considered. Suitable methods will be explained in detail but it must also be remembered by the instructor that teaching does not have to be a formal process, it may be more effective informally, say as a necessary skill in a game.

2.1.5 *Consideration*
This is related to the quality of patience but goes a little deeper in taking into account specific circumstances that may reduce the trainee's learning ability. It involves discreetly finding out the reasons for any problems and taking these into consideration in the tasks being set for the trainee.

2.1.6 *Enthusiasm*
It should be obvious to the trainee that the instructor is enthusiastic about diving and SSAC. This quality is 'infectious' and should help inspire the trainee to greater efforts. Conversely, if a negative attitude is detected by the trainee, then motivation is correspondingly difficult.

2.1.7 *Adaptability*
Apart from being able to vary the method of teaching, the instructor should be able to cope with changing circumstances such as lack of expected equipment, an unexpected change in the weather (for outside activities) or variation in the expected personnel present.

2.1.8 *Fairness*
Trainees sometimes feel that they have to compete for an instructor's attention and time. If favouritism seems apparent to other trainees, then this will adversely affect their enthusiasm. Equally, in considering the criteria for successful completion of a set task, the instructor has to be fair and not let personal feelings influence his assessment of performance. Fairness is important to gain respect from the trainees.

2.1.9. *Knowledge*
The instructor should have a good knowledge in depth (!) of his subject such that any reasonable question can be answered. It may be that

the answer cannot be supplied immediately but the instructor should be able to know where to find the required information.

2.1.10 *Experience*
A wide and varied experience in diving is a great resource for interesting personal accounts that may be recalled to illustrate specific points. Sometimes, a lesson learned by the instructor from his/her personal experience and recounted, may be long remembered by the trainee.

2.2 *Role*

2.2.1 *'Must nots'*
Regard himself as complete and perfect with nothing more to learn.

Regard himself as automatically above others.

'Pull the ladder up behind' by insisting on unreasonable high standards that he/she did not have to achieve, in an effort of self preservation.

2.2.2 *Within the branch*
For basic branch training, covering all theoretical and practical aspects up to 2nd class standard.

To develop and maintain a uniform appropriate standard of instruction and diving throughout SSAC, both by teaching and example.

To assist the Branch Diving Officers (BDOs) to improve diver training.

To run other courses as the instructor gains in their own qualifications, say in boathandling or lifesaving.

To help qualify themselves for branch committee posts such as BDO or Training Officer.

To assist in the attraction of new members into the diving world by providing safe and enjoyable training.

To provide an educated and responsible source of opinion whose attitude will help safeguard SSAC's good name in the eyes of the general public.

2.2.3 *Outside the Branch*
Ideal people for public demonstrations or introductory courses.

Assist local sports councils to cater for the sport diver.

LECTURE 3

The Training Schedule and its Interpretation

3.1 *Introduction*
The Training Schedule is the organised sequence of skills and tests that comprise the SSAC training scheme. It is described in the small record book supplied to all new SSAC members. This book contains much valuable information regarding safe diving practice and is the result of over 37 years of continuous development and revision. Instructors need to be familiar with its contents.

The interpretation of the training described in the schedule is of great importance. The instructor should be aware of the structure within the training schedule and the reasons for teaching the various skills. This interpretation must include an understanding of the purpose behind each skill and knowing what is an acceptable standard of skill acquisition.

Getting signatures in the Training Schedule is not the sole point of training (although some trainees may feel it is). The training record within the schedule indicates the acquisition of the various skills and is almost incidental to the purpose of training. In other words, the training schedule is NOT a test schedule.

The sequence of training within SSAC consists of a logical progression such that it produces safe, competent divers who are well equipped to enjoy their sport. The training of each skill is flexible but the testing of the skill is not; it is specific to the minimum standard required. Such standards are important and must be maintained, while being related to practical diving experience.

3.2 *Parallelism*
Diver training consists of three main areas, theory, pool and open water work. The practical and the theoretical aspects should be taught in parallel so that the trainee can relate one to the other. Most of the theory is taught by formal lessons (or lectures) although there is no firm segregation. Thus some theoretical instruction may be given outside the lecture room and conversely some practical instruction may be given on land.

3.2.1 *Snorkel diver*

Practical skills	Theory (lecture)

Swimming
To demonstrate stamina and some basic ability in the water under slight stress.

Basic snorkel
To demonstrate competence with basic equipment and suitable buoyancy aid, spatial awareness, some breath holding stamina and good finning technique.

Advanced snorkel
To demonstrate overall competence in snorkelling ability combined with rescue skills.

Open water snorkel
To demonstrate similar skills as in Advanced Snorkel but using a diving suit in open water conditions.

1. Training organisation
2. Basic equipment and snorkel diving techniques
3. Ears and sinuses
4. Respiration, hyperventilation, anoxia and hypoxia
5. Rescue, lifesaving and artificial respiration
6. Signals and surfacing drill
7. Exhaustion, protective clothing and hypothermia
8. Description and use of life jackets (and buoyancy compensators)

3.2.2 *Aqualung diver training*

Practical skills	Theory (lecture)

3rd Class
Basic aqualung
To demonstrate some knowledge, competence and ability in the use of the aqualung in the pool, including a simulated recovery from a boat.

Advanced aqualung
To demonstrate more advanced aqualung techniques including co-operation with a buddy and diver rescue.

Pre-open water simulated dive
To demonstrate; ability to safely use aqualung gear, diver signals, demonstrate rescue skills and be ready for open water using full equipment in the pool.

Open water diving
To gain experience in a variety of conditions and to demonstrate competence in basic diving skills in the open water, including rescue techniques.

1. Effects of pressure
2. Principles of the aqualung
3. Aqualung use and buoyancy control
4. Burst lung and ascent in emergency
5. Air endurance and air cylinders
6. Maintenance of equipment and diving accessories
7. Open water diving and dive procedures
8. Decompression, hazards and avoidance

3.2.3 *Advanced aqualung diver*

Practical skills	Theory (lecture)

2nd Class
Qualifying dives
   On-going throughout this course to gain
   experience of a wide range of dive types, problems
   and solutions.

Dive leader
   To demonstrate leadership in a small group.

Expedition leader
   To demonstrate leadership in a moderate sized
   group by organising and managing an expedition
   safely.

Advanced personal skills
   Sweep search.
   Use of surface marker buoy.
   Use of compass.
   Swim without a mask.
   Rescue drill.
   Assisted ascents, 20 and 30m.
   Removing and refitting aqualung Mask, demand
   valve and signals drill.

1. Safety and emergency procedure

2. Nitrogen absorption and narcosis

3. Decompression (advanced)

4. Oxygen, carbon monoxide and carbon dioxide poisoning

5. Underwater navigation and search methods

6. Basic seamanship

7. Expedition organisation

8. Compressor operation

LECTURE 4

Communication Skills and Lecture Preparation
(30-40 min)

4.1 *Introduction*

For any course of instruction, be it in the classroom, pool or open water, there are four main sections. They are; planning, preparation, presentation and review. Good communication is greatly helped by a planned and logical approach.

(This lecture is to concentrate on various ways of teaching in a classroom and is especially relevant to teaching theory. When new divers can understand the reasons and physical phenomena underlying the principles of diving, then they are much more likely to make correct decisions when facing unforseen circumstances.

When preparing for the classroom, the instructor must ensure that their own planning is thorough and complete.)

4.1.1 *Planning*

Define clearly the purpose and objectives of teaching in terms of trainee attainment.

Select teaching material carefully having regard to its difficulty, relevance and progression. Analyse the facts and skills required to achieve the objectives.

Plan to involve the trainee actively in the learning process.

Plan to keep the trainee informed of their progress.

Where appropriate, plan revision and practise to reinforce earlier lessons.

Use efficient means of communication.

Teaching aids
75% of learning is by sight
13% is by hearing
12% is by smell, taste and touch.

Therefore the most effective sense to use is sight.

Visual aids:
    Chalkboard (blackboard)
    NOBO type boards
    A0 paper pads on stands
    Magnetic boards
    Prepared diagrams, posters and pictures
    Duplicated sheets, printed material,
      textbooks
    Models, including cutaways
    Equipment

Projectors:
> overhead
> slide
> film (movies)
> television/video/video disk
> computer screens

Audio aids:
> Radio
> Record player
> Tape players
> Talking books

4.1.2 *Preparation*
The material to be presented can be usefully grouped under one of four headings.

1. Facts that are essential for the trainee to know at this stage.
2. Facts that the trainee should know.
3. Facts that the trainee could know if time permits.
4. Facts that are not relevant at this stage.

Obviously, the material in group 1 should be presented early in the presentation, followed by the facts in groups 2 and 3. Once the content has been decided, it is important that the teacher checks the facts for accuracy and if possible have references to the original data. It is also advisable for the teacher to be aware of the bounds of their knowledge so that, if pressed by questions, an honest admission of limitation of knowledge can be given.

Once the material has been defined as above, what is the best way of ensuring that it is presented completely and effectively during the lesson? For trainee instructors, the safest way is to read word for word from a prepared text. This tends to result in a dull performance and loss of eye to eye contact. Other methods are: to prepare a series of sub-headings on a single sheet of paper to act as an aide memoire; a series of cards with essential facts on and not to use notes at all. It is helpful to remember that humour can help a lot in creating a relaxed atmosphere and to restore any flagging attention.

Consider carefully the equipment you will need for the presentation and check it carefully. Also consider what you will do if some of the equipment malfunctions. Teaching time is precious and should not be spent repairing. Having adequate backup and alternative methods of presenting the required information.

4.1.3 *Presentation*
This is a performance for the benefit of the audience. It should be relaxed, confident and polished. Be positive at all times and avoid statements like 'this is very difficult normally' or 'a lot of people have trouble with this' etc.

Avoid distracting personal mannerisms as far as possible. Ask a close friend to watch you while you lecture, with a remit to note any personal mannerisms, then try to minimise their occurrence.

Vary the intonation of the voice and the direction of voice projection. Ensure that you speak to the whole audience and not just to a lucky few. Eye to eye contact is helpful for good communication.

The lecture (or presentation of theoretical material) should be divided into three main parts:

Introduction

Development

Conclusion (including summary)

4.1.4 *Review*
Check the progress of the trainees by any suitable method (e.g. discussion, test papers) and gauge the effectiveness of the lesson. Try to take the attitude that everyone in the teaching process should have gained something, even if it was 'don't do that again' for the teacher. Keep careful records of the lectures and lessons that you give so that a constant state of continual improvement is established.

4.1.5 *Other teaching forums*
The open discussion

Working in groups

Practical demonstrations

LECTURE 5

Instructional Techniques for Practical Skills

5.1 *Task analysis and matching task to trainee's competence*
The emphasis should be on teaching skills and imparting knowledge, not in just passing tests. The tests are merely incidental, really markers that indicate levels of accepted standards of performance. Teaching skills involves a knowledge of the various individual elements that comprise a complete operation (such as ditch and retrieve the aqualung) and a quick and

accurate assessment of a trainee's current level of ability. The instructor then has to match the trainee with an element of the complete operation such that it seems easy and achievable. Once this skill has been acquired by the trainee, then the Instructor should move onto the next element and so on until all the individual elementary skills have been learned. At this stage, sequences of the elementary skills should be linked together in a progressive manner so that the trainee initially attempts say two elementary skills consecutively. Once this has been mastered, then another skill can be added to the sequence and so on until the whole operation has been mastered. Some people learn very rapidly and a first approach may be to demonstrate the complete operation to the trainee (or have it demonstrated), then to ask the trainee to imitate the operation, having due regard to the safety implications. The importance of correct demonstrations cannot be overemphasised enough. If the instructor has any doubt about their own ability in any particular skill, then they should practice until the doubt is removed. It is important for the instructor to be realistic in their own level of performance and if in doubt during a training session, then 'borrow' a more competent body for the demonstration.

5.2 Evidence for acceptable performance
The criterion is to achieve the desired result in a safe and efficient manner. The instructor should not insist on the ultimate in performance but the demonstration of skill so that the trainee accomplishes the desired result in a manner that is effective and does not require undue effort. This may not be achieved in the normal orthodox way but the manner of the achievement may not necessarily matter. Sometimes, the astute instructor may come across a better alternative method to perform a particular task.

5.3 Teaching

5.3.1 Position

5.3.2 Use of alternative ways of achieving the end result
Practical work, discussion, role playing etc. may be effective mechanisms of teaching.

5.3.3 Achievement for trainee important

5.3.4 Encouragement and support for the trainee

5.3.5. Enjoyment the name of the game

5.4 Demonstration
Demonstrations, preceded and followed by explanation, are in many ways the sine qua non of instruction.

5.4.1 Quality all-important

5.4.2 Instructor must practice and be confident

5.5 Detection and correction of faults
Very important and bad practises must not be accepted.

Noticing a fault is one thing but correction may be difficult. Use of task analysis is very helpful as is the use of alternative methods.

5.6 Positive feedback
Essential for both the trainee and the instructor. Try to find some area where progress has been made and emphasise the positive aspects. Try to ensure that when the trainee leaves the session, it is on a high note so that they are keen to return for more. If this is achieved then the instructor will also benefit and leave with a sense of satisfaction.

5.7 Use of games and props
These can be useful to develop skills and physical attributes in an informal manner. Some techniques are described in Ch. 2 of this Manual and are well worth a go. Games like underwater rugby, octopush or collecting pennies from the pool bottom on one breath can be great fun.

LECTURE 6

Snorkel and Aqualung Training

The trainees should be reminded that the Training Schedule states the requirements of training and the Manual (Elementary Training) the purposes of the tests and advice on technique.

Planning
Pool training should be planned with regard to the size, skills and availability of training personnel and the likely numbers of trainees. A booking-in system should be established for use at the pool session. This can be combined with record keeping. Safety requirements and the need for a poolside safety officer should be remembered.

Teaching

Size of trainee groups should be established. As an instructor's ability increases he or she should be able to handle increasingly large groups effectively, but it is unlikely that an instructor however skilled can handle more than four trainees underwater. The Instructional cycle in a pool session normally includes the following in the sequence given below:

Briefing – setting down the objectives, the method and the assessment of the trainees abilities. Break down of training into sensible component stages.

Demonstration – perhaps both above and in the water.

Trainees attempt first exercise (first component).

Success or failure to carry out component successfully. Sensible analytical advice from instructor.

Return to demonstration or to repeat first exercise if attainment was poor. If good instruction proceeds to nest component entering at demonstration stage.

At end of session. Review of attainment. Advice on problems, instructor should always find something praisable. Completion of records.

In the testing mode the only difference is that no Demonstration is given and the trainee proceeds through all exercises laid down for Training Schedule as components of the Test.

LECTURE 7

Record Keeping

Emphasis should be given on the necessity of good record keeping. Good records help instructors plan training, resolve arguments about what training a person has received, provide essential information in the unlikely event of an accident and are proof that a dive group is well-run.

Records should be kept, at the poolside and in the water on slates if necessary. They are essential on a dive in open water and can be initiated as the dive plan and then when diving starts be filled in with dive details. The person in charge of pool training or a dive should normally depute someone to carry out record taking. Branches should use standard forms prepared within the branch, though a dive record form is illustrated in Fig. 78 pp. 45-6.

When training is carried out the record should be used to notify trainees of their progress so that they are quite certain where they are judged to be in the training sequence.

Pool and dive records kept on site should be copied as soon as possible into master records kept by the branch.

LECTURE 8

From Pool to Open Water

8.1 *Introduction*

This lecture is concerned with the instructor's supervision of a diver's first open water dive.

For the trainee, this experience should be exciting, exhilarating and fulfilling. For the instructor, this experience can also be very rewarding for, if the trainee has enjoyed the outing, then normally, they are not slow to convey their sense of enjoyment to the instructor. It is therefore important for the instructor to be especially considerate and understanding, both in the planning and in the actual dive. There are a number of factors that the instructor has to consider in addition to the normal routine ones. The trainee will normally be very apprehensive about the dive so the instructor must try to arrange to minimise any stress felt by the trainee from all other factors as far as possible.

8.2 *Site*

This must be chosen with care having regard to the prevailing weather so that it is sheltered; the seabed and underwater life must be interesting to the trainee; the visibility should be reasonable, say greater than 5 metres; access to the water should be easy with no rock climbing, excessively long hikes or long car journeys on the day; conditions underfoot on the shore should be firm and gently sloping to the water's edge with no sudden drop-offs and these conditions should continue underwater.

A quiet site away from crowds is preferable so that if the trainee makes a mistake of any sort or feels awkward, they do not feel that all the world is watching. Thus the presence of girl/boy friends etc. is to be discouraged on this occasion. Similarly, there should be a minimum of boat traffic and other water sports people in the area.

The conditions underwater should also be relaxing with an absence of currents or tidal streams. Check on the expected state of the tide before arrival at the site so that conditions will be gentle. Have an alternative site if the first one is unsuitable for any reason (it is usually weather).

8.3 *Weather*
Conditions must be calm. If the wind is force 2 or above, reconsider the dive. Ideally the wind should be a dead calm. Avoid temperatures that cause discomfort such as hot summer or cold winter days if possible. The cloud cover is not all that important except if it seriously reduces the available light. Remember that what ever the available light on the surface, it will be significantly reduced underwater. Sea swell should be negligible.

8.4 *Conduct of the dive*
On arrival at the site, brief the trainee in a calm, reassuring and friendly manner. Use the mnemonic, DEEDS as a guide for remembering the areas to cover, namely, **D**iscipline (e.g. position to maintain during the dive, action if separated), **E**xercise (purpose and route of the dive), **E**quipment (e.g. check air contents, buoyancy compensator, instruments, function of regulators), **D**angers (e.g. breath out during ascents, clear ears on descent) and **S**ignals. Do not over elaborate and keep the briefing as simple as possible. Do not attempt any tests on this dive.

Help the trainee during kitting up without fussing. Ensure that the equipment is put on in the correct order. Try to keep the formalities to a minimum that is consistant with safety. Remember to ask the trainee to check your equipment. After kitting up, briefly go over the dive plan again, turn on each other's air and check in with the beach marshall and safety officer. Ensure that there is spare lead available close at hand for the trainee's first task in the water is to achieve neutral buoyancy.

The instructor should lead the way into the water by fitting the fins and walking backwards. Take plenty of time and let the trainee progress at a gentle pace. Help them to achieve neutral buoyancy at the surface, avoid a long snorkel swim to the descent point and commence the dive.

Do not go deeper than 10 metres. Keep close contact and encourage frequent checking of air contents. A trainee's first dives air con-

sumption will probably be their greatest of their diving career so keep a close watch on it. They may well tend to breathe very deeply causing positive buoyancy problems in the shallow depths. If such problems cause the trainee any distress, surface under control and wait for them to calm down. It may be necessary to return to waist deep water for them to regain their feet and composure.

Sometimes a trainee will forget to equalise their air pressure in their mask, resulting in the 'red eye syndrome' caust by burst blood vessels on the eye. Early symptoms of this are the mask being flattened against the face. If this happens, stop at the current depth or ascent slightly and allow the trainee time to remedy the situation.

Assuming that the dive is progressing as planned, remember to point out as much of the underwater features and wildlife as possible for it will all be new to the trainee and will probably be of great interest. Do not attempt to swim quickly or for any great distance. Keep a close check on the condition of the trainee, in particular, watch the eyes! Any sign of staring eyes and/or lack of response to signals will probably indicate that the trainee is experiencing excessive stress. If this is evident, then surface under control and try tactfully to discover the problem. When the trainee's air supply is down to about one third capacity remaining, it is time to surface. Give the signal to surface and ensure that it is acknowledged. Face each other on the way up and check for obstructions above during the ascent. Make sure that the trainee vents off their dry suit and/or buoyancy aid as required to maintain the correct rate to the surface. Once at the surface, signal 'OK' to the shore party and swim ashore. Lead the trainee to the shore but let them exit from the sea first. Check in with the beach marshal and get changed as soon as possible without rushing.

8.5 *After the dive*
If it is cold, get some warm drink for both of you and encourage the trainee to talk of the dive. It is a magic moment, the completion of the first open water dive so let them enthuse about it (if appropriate!). Ensure that they complete their dive log, you complete yours and sign each others log books. (Remember the good examples for the trainee to model on.) Try to make sure that the trainee's dive experience ends on a high note so that they are impatient to return to the open water.

LECTURE 9

Decompression Considerations

The lecture should follow the outlines set out in Chapter 3 of the sister Manual. Trainees should be encouraged to work through examples of single dives and repetitive dives requiring decompression. Particular attention should be given to situations where the ascent rate is non-standard. Trainees should be taught the supreme importance of avoiding getting into decompression requiring situations and to have a good knowledge of possible symptoms of decompression sickness as well as the procedures to be followed with suspected cases of decompression sickness.

LECTURE 10

Assessment Procedures for Branch Instructors

Assessment is part of the procedure of training for Branch Instructor and it is both a check on standards and an act of support.

The assessments should have been completed within one year of the training course. The candidate will be examined in lecture technique, their ability to instruct 2/3 snorkel trainees and up to 2 aqualung trainees, firstly in a pool locality and then in an open water locality. The pool instruction is to be taken from the pool training schedule. The open water instruction is to be taken from the 3rd or 2nd class open water training schedule.

Pool and open water work to be assessed by one examiner, preferably with the Regional Coach present.

It is suggested that candidates apply for assessment 6 months after the training course, either by writing to the Examinations Co-ordinator, your Regional Coach or the course organiser. All assessment requests are routed through the Examinations Co-ordinator who arranges for the examiners to be available and maintains the records of instructors and examiners. Once the process is complete, a unique Branch Instructor number is issued to the candidate who may quote this number after signing up tests etc. All awards must then be ratified by the NDC and General Committee before training schedules are endorsed by the NDO and Chairman.

10.1 *Assessment in detail*
The candidate will be given the resources, trainees and a request to teach a certain skill. The examiner will discretely stay in the background and will not need to be considered at all by the instructor candidate.

10.1.1 *Organisation for pool/open water*
   Safety
   Resources
   Time
   Records
   Teaching position

10.1.2 *Teaching for pool/open water*
   Briefing
   Assessment of group's ability
   Task Objective(s) decided
   Demonstrations
   Detection and correction of faults
   Task analysed or generalised
   De-briefing
   Recording of results of training

10.1.3 *General points for examiners*
(in addition to above)
   Instructor's use of reinforcement
      (informative and encouraging)
   Skills achieved in relation to task
      objectives
   Mandatory pass

10.1.4 *Assessment de-brief*
This usually takes place in a quiet, friendly atmosphere when the candidate, examiner and Regional Coach can discuss the lesson(s) in detail. At the end of this discussion, the examiner will explain his/her decisions with reasons. The whole process should be supportive and constructive leaving the candidate with a feeling of significant achievement.

PRACTICAL TRAINING AND ASSOCIATED LECTURES

COMPRESSOR OPERATION

Aim
To teach a person how to use a high-pressure air compressor (fixed or portable) and storage bank for recharging compressed air diving cylinders safely and effectively.

Teaching Method
The trainee must first attend a lecture on the

principles and practice of compressor operation. Then,

(a) The trainee will receive a practical demonstration of the operation of at least two types of compressor, one of which must be used in connection with a storage bank and manifold decanting system. The trainee should then practice these skills under supervision.

(b) Then the trainee will demonstrate his or her competence by a practical examination and his or her theoretical knowledge by a short multi-choice question paper. The examiner shall be a Club Examiner.

Theoretical knowledge
Properties of compressed air, pressure, volume and temperature changes on compression, changes in water vapour state, condensation.

Electric motor, petrol engine, diesel engine drives. Compressor construction. Piston stages, intercooling, dewatering, filtration. Charging panels, high pressure pipework. Safety.

Marking of cylinders, their meanings relative to filling.

Air testing.

Practical knowledge
Start-up and stopping procedures. Sequence of operation of valves. Draining of condensed water/oil. Filter changing. Air purity testing. Correct reading and actions in respect of cylinder markings. Logging operations.

BOAT-HANDLING AND SEAMANSHIP

Aim
To teach and check that a diver is wholly competent in using a small hard-boat, inflatable or rigid-hulled inflatable safely in support of diving.

Note that the RYA Sport-Boat Handling Course plus 20 hours of practical experience may be taken in lieu of the course outlined below. The examination shall be that outlined below.

Teaching method
Theory: By lectures. It is envisaged that the lecture course should be completed in five to six lectures over four hours total time. The trainee should also work through examples of tidal height calculation, current strength and direction calculation, trip calculation (taking effects of current into account) in a work book.

Practical. By experience with boats, with one to three hours under the supervision of an instructor and then a further twenty hours of practical experience in a suitable boat.

Theoretical knowledge
Types of boats, their advantages and disadvantages. Types of motor. Equipment to be carried in a boat. Launching, beaching, anchoring, manoeuvres, dropping divers, picking up divers, effects of sea and wind on a boat. Rules of the road. Simple navigation, chart use, tide-tables, current data, transits, more advanced position fixing, Safety and rescue.

Practical knowledge
Launching, starting an engine, getting underway, running at speed appropriate to sea, load and direction. Anchoring, picking up a floating object, tieing up onto a buoy, dropping/picking up divers, return to shore.

Dealing with simple engine problems. Loss of connection of fuel line, carburettor flooding, replacing propellor, breakage of engine cut-out, breakage of recoil start (if fitted). Diagnosis of more serious faults, including loss of cooling, loss of ignition, salt water entering carburettor.

Examination
An examination of theoretical knowledge by a multi-choice question paper, at least 50 questions. A practical examination of at least one hour duration in a boat. Examiners, RYA Examiners or Approved SSAC Club Examiners.

BIBLIOGRAPHY

Although almost any book about diving will be of some value to the diver who wants to learn we particularly recommend the following books.

1. *Diving Manuals. (Elementary to moderately advanced.)*

Sport Diving. The British Sub-Aqua Club Diving Manual. 11th Edition. 1985 (or later). Stanley Paul, London. ISBN 0 09 163861 3.

A very useful if rather bulky text that takes you most of the way from the most basic features of diving to 1st Class Diver standard. Rather expensive. Very good on basic physics and equipment.

Advanced Sport Diving. 1990. Stanley Paul, London. ISBN 0 09 173828 8. Pp. 160.

Covers much the same material as the second part of the SSAC Training Manual, in much the same detail, though it is more heavily sectionalised. It does, however, contain a small section on UW explosives!

Underwater Diving. Basic techniques. By Peter Dick and David Sisman. 1986. Pelham Books, London. ISBN 0 7207 1664 0.

An introduction to the sport taking you to a level slightly below SSAC 3rd Class. A companion volume *Advanced Diving* is planned. Recommended by the Sub-Aqua Association.

Sport Diving. The complete manual for skin and scuba divers. By A. P. Balder. 1978. Collier, New York. ISBN 0 02 028140 4.

A cheaply produced book which covers the basics well.

Easy Diving. By Lou Fead. 1985. Underwater World Publications, London. ISBN 0 946020 05 1.

The title describes it perfectly!

Advanced Sports Diving. A to Z. By D. Graver. 1976. No publisher declared. Lib. of Congress No. 739710.

'Advanced' again means 2nd Class. A useful book.

This is Sport Diving Technique. By D. Marcante. 1978. Nautical Publishing Co., Lymington. ISBN 0 245 52862 8.

A well-illustrated elementary manual. Very good on use of ABLJs.

PADI Manual. Published by Professional Association of Diving Instructors.

A very detailed manual of excellent quality.

The training corresponds fairly closely to SSAC procedures.

Scuba Diving. The adventure Series. By Anneka Rice. 1988. Robson Books, London. ISBN 0 86051 463 3.

A straightforward guide to elementary aspects of diving. It accompanies a video of the same title.

The complete Scuba Diving Guide. By Dave Saunders. Photography by Mike Portelly. 1987. A. & C. Black, London. ISBN 0 7136 5536 4.

Complete? Pretty nearly for elements of scuba diving!

Sport Diver Manual. 1975. Jeppesen, Denver. ISBN 0 88487 009 X.

A manual, prepared by a writing team, which is very clearly presented. Oriented to USA practice but little the worse for that. Takes the reader to something roughly equivalent to 3rd Class standard. A tape slide set and a book of advice for instructors is also available to complement this book.

Sport Diver Manual – advanced open water activities. 1979. Jeppesen, Denver. ISBN 0 88487 054 5.

'Advanced' means 2nd Class in our parlance. A very useful book.

Advanced Wreck Diving Guide. By Gary Gentile. 1988. Pp. viii + 136. Cornell Maritime Press, Centreville, Maryland. ISBN 0 87033 380 1.

A detailed and very sensible book obviously written from much personal experience.

2. *Advanced Diving. Professional manuals. Codes of Practice etc.*

The diving manuals of the various navies and codes of practice for scientific diving etc. give much valuable information on the most advanced techniques that amateur divers will use as well as still more interesting but not wholly relevant information on matters such as mixed gas diving.

Principles of Diving. By Mark Terrell. 1965. Stanley Paul, London. Pp. 240.

A slightly elderly book but still excellent in many ways because it does cover the basic principles of physics, physiology and seamanship that a diver must know. The descriptions of commercial and naval equipment are mainly of historical interest.

Code of practice for scientific diving. 1974. Underwater Association. Edited by N. C. Flemming and D. L. Miles.

This book is not a manual but contains much

sensible advice on the more advanced types of diving that a scuba diver might need to know. Well worth consulting if you plan an expedition or a difficult or demanding type of dive.

CIRIA Code of practice
The principles of safe diving practice. 1972. Ciria-UEG, London. ISBN 0 901208 26 4.

Ciria is the acronym for the Construction Industrial Research and Information Association and the booklet is intended for those working in commercial diving.

US Navy Diving Manual. Volume 1. Air Diving. 0994-LP-001-9010. (Obtain the latest update possible but do not accept any issue prior to December 1975 except for historical purposes.)

Though this is intended for USN personnel the description of air diving contains much of value to the beginner. Note that the USN uses scuba in much the same way as sports divers (unlike the RN).

US Navy Diving Manual. Volume 2. Mixed Gas Diving. 0994-LP-001-9010. September 1973 or later updates.

This volume is not primarily relevant to sports divers though they may find it very interesting reading. Rapid development of USN equipment makes it desirable to obtain a recent update.

Diving Manual BR 2806. 1972. Ministry of Defence. ISBN 011 771345 7.

Though this manual contains much of interest and value to the sports diver it is written for the training of RN personnel in types of diving which differ considerably from that undertaken by SSAC members. Does not describe RN equipment in any great detail. Contains full RN decompression tables.

The Professional Diver's Handbook. Edited by David Sisman. 1982. Submex, London. ISBN 0 9508242 0 8.

A collection of articles related to commercial deep diving practice. Rapid developments in the field are tending to make it look dated.

La plongee et l'intervention sous la mer. By Y. Berry, P. Gavarry and others. 1977. Arthaud, France.

No excuse for mentioning a French book. This one tells you a lot about the French approach to commercial and naval diving.

Plongee – Loisir en securité. By P. Molle. 1989. Editions amphora, Paris. ISBN 2 85180 184 1.

A very good guide to the application of the current French Decompression Tables which are very safe. Also contains much other good training material. In French.

3. *Diving Physiology*

The physiology and medicine of diving and compressed air work. 1975. By P. B. Bennett and D. H. Elliott. 1975. 2nd Edition. Balliere-Tindall, London. ISBN 0 7020 0538 X.

An expensive and comprehensive but advanced textbook. You need a moderate knowledge of the subject before you can appreciate it.

Underwater Medicine. By S. Miles and D. E. MacKay. 1976. 4th Edition. Granada Publications, London. ISBN 0 229 11559 4.

A book which is fairly easily understood by those untrained in physiology. Slightly out of date.

The Underwater Handbook. Edited by C. W. Schilling. M. F. Watts and N. Schandemeier. 1976. Plenum, New York. ISBN 0 306 30843 6.

This underwater physiology textbook is intended for engineers rather than medical experts so it is rather more easily read by the non-expert than the other two books.

Note that many diving manuals (see above) have fairly adequate sections on diving physiology.

The Diver's Medical Companion. By Robert Thomas and Bart McKenzie. Undated but about 1977. Australian Sports Publications. ISBN 0 86895 048 3.

Fairly simply written.

4. *Boatmanship and Navigation*

Coastwise Navigation. Notes for Yachtsmen. By G. G. Watkins. 1972 (or later). Kandy Publications, Sevenoaks. ISBN 0 85309 009 2.

Marine Chartwork and Navaids. By D. A. Moore. 1981. Kandy Publications, Sevenoaks. ISBN 0540 072699.

Safety and Survival at sea. By E. C. B. Lee and Kenneth Lee. 1971. Cassell, London. ISBN 0 304 93719 3.

Advice on what to do to prevent drowning or hypothermia, to treat these conditions and how to abandon a sinking craft as well as much other advice.

Inflatable Boats. By G. W. R. Nicholl. 1969. Adlard Coles, London. ISBN 0 229 69301 1.

The Seaway Code. Published by Department of Trade. Revised frequently.

Knots and splices. By Cyrus L. Day. 1953. Adlard Coles, London. ISBN 0 229 642349.

The inflatable boat book. By Kendall McDonald and Malcolm Todd. 1975. ISBN 7207 0833 8.

Seamanship for Divers. 1986. Pp. 160. Stanley Paul, London. ISBN 0 09 166291 5.

The BSAC's manual on boathandling. Written in their now standard heavily sectionalised style but the slices are mostly tasty. A little short on detail about navigation.

5. Marine Biology

There are a vast number of books in this area most of them of at least some value. If you want to know what animals you have seen while diving (or indeed what plants) we recommend the following four books. The fifth book is an excellent introduction to the science of marine biology.

The Hamlyn guide to the seashore and shallow seas of Britain and Europe. By A. C. Campbell. Illustrated by James Nichols. 1976. Hamlyn, London. ISBN 0 600 34396 0.

British Seafishes. By Frances Dipper. 1987. Underwater World Publications, London. ISBN 946020 13 2.

Fishes of the sea. By John and Gillian Lythgoe. 1971. Blandford, London. ISBN 0 7137 0539 6.

Good for identifying UK and Mediterranean fish.

Oxford book of invertebrates. By D. Nichols and J. Cooke. 1971. Oxford, London. ISBN 0 19 91000 8X.

Good illustrations and a simple text but you need to know roughly what you are trying to identify in order to find the right page.

Oxford Book of flowerless plants. By Brightman. 1966. Oxford, London. ISBN 0 19 91000 47.

Good for identifying seaweeds.

An introduction to Marine Science. By P. S. Meadows and J. I. Campbell. 1978. Blackie, Glasgow and London. ISBN 0 216 90592 3.

Once you want really to understand what goes on in the sea this is the book to turn to, comprehensive and well written.

Guide to Inshore Marine Life. By David Ernia and Bernard Picton. 1987. Immel Publishing, London. ISBN 0 907151 345.

A useful brief book.

6. Salvage

Boatman's guide to light salvage. By G. N. Reid. 1979. Cornell Maritime Press. Centreville, Maryland. ISBN 0 87033 248.

An excellent book but note that the chapter on legal aspects deals with salvage law in the USA not in the UK.

Nautical Archaeology. By Bill St John Wilkes. 1971. David and Charles, Newton Abbot. ISBN 0 7153 5023 4.

Despite the title of this book it is all about underwater work, work indeed which might be used in archaeology but which is also most useful in salvage. A lot of detail on lifting methods.

7. Archaeology

Archaeology under water. By George F. Bass. 1970. Pelican Books, Harmondsworth. ISBN none recorded.

A History of Seafaring based on underwater archaeology. Edited by George F. Bass. Book Club Associates, London. 1974. ISBN none recorded.

Maritime Archaeology. By Keith Muckleroy. 1978. Cambridge University Press, Cambridge. ISBN 0 521 29348 0 (paperback).

A good discussion of the general relevance of this area of study for historical studies and also of what happens to artefacts as a boat is wrecked and thereafter.

8. Underwater Photography

Underwater photography for everyone. By Flip Schulke. 1979. Prentice-Hall, New York. ISBN 0 13 936450 1.

This text is oriented towards specific commercial underwater cameras which are widely available to the amateur photographer.

A Manual of underwater photography. By T. Glover, G. E. Harwood and J. N. Lythgoe. 1977. Academic Press, London and New York. ISBN 0 12 286750 5.

If you are interested in the scientific approach to photography underwater this is the text for you. Also good on advice on making housings.

Underwater Photography, Movies and still. By Derek Townsend. 1971 2nd Edition. George Allen and Unwin, London. ISBN 0 04 778001 0.

An elementary text.

9. *Miscellaneous*

Accidents happen. By Ann Welch. 1979. John Murray, London. ISBN 0 7195 3552 2.

A thought provoking book which should make you take thought to reduce the chance of your having a diving (or other) accident.

Life Saving, Water Safety. The Royal Life Saving Society, London. No ISBN number. Obtain latest edition.

Life Saving and Water Safety Handbook. 1978. 4th Edition. The Royal Life Saving Society, London. Published in 8 sections. No ISBN number.

Swimming free. By Geoffrey Fraser Dutton. 1972. Wm. Heinemann, London. ISBN 0 434 21920 7.

A paean to the joys of snorkelling – especially in Scottish waters.

Clyde Shipwrecks. By Peter Moir and Ian Crawford. 1988. Moir Crawford, Wemyss Bay. ISBN 0 9513366 0 6.

Dive North-West Scotland. By Gordon Ridley. 1985. Underwater World Publications, London. ISBN 0 946020 04 3.

Appendices

A ROPED DIVER AND BUDDY LINE SIGNALS

Rope signals can be given by a diver to an attendant on the surface or vice-versa, on a lifeline or a surface marker line. They can also be given between one diver and another if a buddy line is used. In all cases the line should be reasonably taut before the signal is given. If it is slack the signal will simply disappear in a few metres as the slack in the line is pulled in. Thus if you are using rope signal systems always keep the line fairly taut by paying out or pulling in line as appropriate. The surface attendant pays out or pulls in line to his diver; the dive leader pays out or pulls in buddy lines and the dive leader keeps the line to a surface float taut. Note that signals on surface float lines can only be initiated by the surface attendant in a boat coming up to the float and starting signalling.

A simple roped diver signalling system is as follows and is also used by BSAC.

Signal	Surface attendant	Diver
ONE PULL	Are you OK?	I am OK
TWO PULLS	Stay put	I am stationary
THREE PULLS	Descend	I want to descend
FOUR PULLS	Come up	I am ascending
CONTINUOUS PULLS	Emergency Surface immediately	Emergency Pull me up

When using a buddy line two of the signals are changed as follows:

THREE PULLS	Move away from me
FOUR PULLS	Come to me

All signals should be acknowledged. For instance three pulls from the diver would be answered by three pulls from the attendant unless he did not wish the diver to descend, in which case he might use two pulls. If a signal is unacknowledged after a reasonable interval for response it should be repeated and if it is still unacknowledged by a diver the Dive Marshal should be informed since he may wish to send down a stand-by diver. The RN and commercial companies have a more complex rope signal system, see BSAC diving manuals or Royal Navy Diving Manual.

B OTHER SIGNALS

Diving Flag. Flag A flown while divers are down. The following pages of the Manual deal with the types of signalling listing below:

Introductory Manual	
Surface signals for snorkellers	28
Hand signals for divers	55-57

Torch signals for night diving this book 67
Distress signals for boats are described on page 49 but we repeat them in full here:

In daylight:
A yellow smoke flare (orange coloured smoke is also acceptable).
The International Code Flags letters **N C**.
An ensign hoisted upside down.
Slowly raising and lowering outstretched arms repeatedly.
A coat or article of clothing displayed on an oar or mast.
A signal consisting of a square flag hoisted with a ball or anything resembling a ball above or below it.
An ensign made fast high in the rigging.

At night, dusk, dawn or in poor light:
A rocket parachute flare or hand flare showing a red light.
Flames on the vessel, e.g., burning an oily rag.
A torch or lamp signal repeating the SOS signal.

At all times:
The continuous sounding of a whistle or siren.
An SOS signal by whistle.
Use of radio to signal **SOS** or **MAYDAY**.
Use channel 16 for distress calls. If the situation

primarily calls for medical assistance call **PANMED.**

Divers may also use the smoke and/or red light flare if in distress on the surface.

C DECOMPRESSION TABLES

See current logbooks or cards issued by SSAC. The RNPL 1975 Tables are used. BSAC 88 or other tables are not used.

D RECOMPRESSION CHAMBERS

See details in current logbooks. Changes are reported in the 'Announcement' section of the club magazine, *Scottish Diver*.

E SEA STATES AND WIND FORCE

See details in current logbooks.

F COASTGUARD STATIONS (SCOTLAND)

Southernness (Dumfries) to Girvan. HQ at Ramsay, IOM.
Tel: 0624 813255.

Clyde Area. Girvan to Crinan. HQ at Greenock.
Tel: 0475 29014 or 29988.

Oban Area. Crinan to Loch Torridon. HQ at Oban. Tel: 0631 63720 or 63729.

Stornoway Area. Loch Torridon to limit at 320° from Cape Wrath. HQ at Stornoway.
Tel: 0851 2013.

Pentland Area. Cape Wrath to Moray Firth Ord Point. HQ at Kirkwall.
Tel: 0856 3268.

Aberdeen Area. From Ord Point to Red Head. HQ at Aberdeen.
Tel: 0224 52275.

Forth Area. Red Head to Berwick on Tweed.
Tel: 0333 50666.

Shetland. Lerwick.
Tel: 0595 2976.

G WEATHER FORECASTS

Available from coastguard stations.

Available with expert advice from Glasgow Weather Centre. Tel. 041-248 3451 for all parts of Scotland.

Radio – Weekdays
Shipping forecasts are broadcast on the following BBC transmissions: 198 kHz (1500 metres) at 05.55, 13.55, 17.50, 00.33. 00.38 (Inshore).

Weather forecasts (landsman oriented) are broadcast on Radio 3 at 6.55, and on Radio 4 at 05.55, 07.55, 12.55, 17.55, and 00.20 and Radio Scotland 810 kHz at 05.55, 06.28, 09.02, 10.02, 12.58, 17.58, 21.58 (Monday to Friday). Frequencies used vary locally.

Sundays
Shipping forecasts on 200 kHz at the same times as on weekdays. Weather forecasts on Radio 3 at 6.55 and on Radio 4 at 6.55, 7.55 (200 kHz only), 8.55, 12.55, 17.55 (200 kHz only) and 00.20 (approx.).

Television forecasts are transmitted at the end of the main News programmes on BBC 1 and ITV. The BBC 1 forecast at approx. 18.30 (Mondays to Fridays) is generally the most detailed forecast of the day also at 12.12 and 21.31. On Sundays it is usually transmitted at 18.40 approx. and at somewhat variable times on Saturdays. ITN forecasts after News. Breakfast TV has frequent summary forecasts on Channels 1 and 3.

H MINIMUM SIZES FOR SHELLFISH

The Immature Crabs and Lobsters order 1976 specifies that crabs of the species *Cancer pagurus* cannot be landed, sold or in possession for sale if the width across the broadest part of the shell is 115mm or less. It also specifies that lobsters shall not be sold, landed or in possession for sale if the length along the carapace, measured from the rear of either eye socket to the rear end of the body shell along a line parallel to the centre line of the body shell is 80mm or less.

Index

This index is to both the Introductory and to the Advanced Manual. Page numbers for the Introductory Manual are set in normal type, those to the Advanced Manual in bold type e.g. **126.**